GUIDE TO ANCIENT ROME

GUIDE TO ANCIENT ROME

Ada Gabucci

MONDADORI

CONTENTS

1 The Valley of the Colosseum 7

2 The Palatine and the Circus Maximus 21

3 The Roman Forum 43

4 The Imperial Forums 61

5 From the Campus Martius to the Mausoleum of Hadrian 77

6 Public Works 105

7 The Museums 127

Appendix

Where to Eat and Where to Stay 137

Statue of a Vestal Virgin and Temple
of Antoninus and Faustina, Roman
Forum.

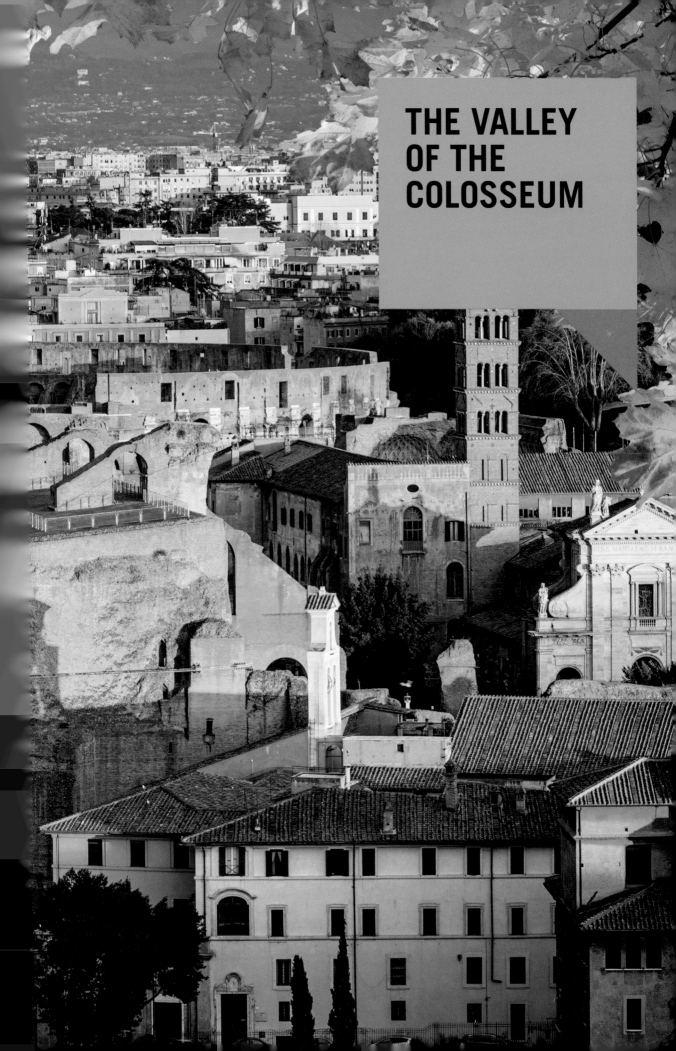

THE VALLEY OF THE COLOSSEUM

On the previous pages
View of the Colosseum.

Colosseum, cells,
passageway with hoists.

Detail of the Colosseum
in a watercolour by L.J. Duc
(1802–1879). Ecole des
Beaux. Arts, Paris.

The Colosseum.

HISTORY

"As long as the Colosseum stands Rome shall stand.
When the Colosseum falls Rome shall fall with it."
(Venerable Bede, eighth century)

Until the nineteenth century the open space now named
Piazza del Colosseo was a valley ringed round with five
hills, the Palatine, Velia, Fagutal, Oppian and Caelius. In
antiquity the area was originally occupied by houses;
but in 64 AD the Emperor Nero took it in hand. After a
fire ravaged the hillsides he incorporated it into the
construction of his immense and sumptuous palace,
significantly named the Domus Aurea or Golden House.
At the entrance to the Domus Aurea stood a gigantic
bronze statue, 32 metres high, of Nero as the Sun God,
an imitation of the celebrated Colossus of Rhodes. The
statue was spared by Vespasian, though he demolished
all other traces of his predecessor's megalomania. Vespasian restored the valley to public use and began to
work on the amphitheatre called the Colosseum after
Nero's colossal statue.
In the same period, a monumental fountain stood in the
area now in front of the Arch of Constantine, a later work.
The water gushed out of a conical fountain 17 metres
high into a basin 16 metres across. Its shape, rather like

the conical pillars that marked the turn in the chariot races, with the water pouring down its sides, earned it the name of the Meta Sudans or Sweating Pillar.

The present state of Piazza del Colosseo is the result of demolition work in 1932 on the construction of Via dell'Impero and Via dei Trionfi (now Via dei Fori Imperiali and Via di San Gregorio). This entailed the levelling of the Velia and destruction of the last imposing remains of the Meta Sudans and the base of Nero's Colossus.

Colosseum, aerial view.

The Colosseum: detail of a model. Museo della Civiltà Romana, Rome.

Vespasian (68–79 AD). Museo Nazionale Romano, Rome.

THE COLOSSEUM

Construction of the Colosseum as an arena for public shows was begun by the Emperor Vespasian and completed by his son Titus. He inaugurated it in 80 AD with games lasting for a hundred days, at which 5000 wild beasts were slain.

Under the empire the Colosseum was extensively repaired a number of times following fires and earthquakes. On 23 August, 217 AD it was repeatedly struck by lightning and all the wooden structures, which included the floor of the arena, went up in the blaze. The city's seven firefighting battalions and sailors from the fleet at Misenus failed to quell the flames. The Colosseum remained unserviceable for some years but in 223 the Emperor Alexander Severus restored it to its ancient splendour. Despite the efforts of Constantine and his successors to abolish gladiatorial combats, they were finally banned only in 404 by Honorius. For over a century thereafter the only entertainments were combats with wild animals. The last spectacle was presented in 523.

History of the Excavations

The loss of the Colosseum's original function as an arena led to its progressive decay and alteration. It was stripped of its metal fittings and the stone was carted away for reuse as building material. But the edifice was never completely abandoned: between the twelfth and thirteenth centuries it was incorporated into the fortress of the Frangipane family, and in the sixteenth century the arena was consecrated and a chapel built on it.

In the seventeenth and eighteenth centuries greater interest in preserving relics of the past led to a ban on the removal of stone for building material.

The first systematic excavations began in the nineteenth century and revealed the structures below the arena. There was extensive restoration. Since then, the Colosseum has been the focus of scholars' interest and subjected to numerous campaigns of excavation and restoration. For some time now there has been discussion about the advisability of reconstructing the floor of the arena, with the creation of a route for visits to the underground areas.

Interior of the Colosseum

Sixty-six numbered entrances led to the three tiers of seating. The amphitheatre could be shaded by an immense awning hoisted by a squad of sailors from the fleet at Misenus. At the two sides of the smaller axis of the arena there were honorary stands for the emperor, consuls, Vestal Virgins, and other court dignitaries. The topmost tier of the amphitheatre provided standing room for the poorest classes. The arena itself was an oval measuring 86 meters across its longer axis. Its surface was a deck of wooden boards covering a dense network of tunnels which contained the scenery, hoists and pens for wild animals. The Colosseum could comfortably hold a crowd of 50,000 (today, the San Siro Stadium in Milan holds a crowd of 80,000) and the spectacles lasted several hours.

Wild Beasts and Gladiators

Professional gladiators were very popular. They might be free men or slaves (who sometimes won their freedom by their victories in the arena) and they

The Colosseum and the Arch of Constantine in a painting by Canaletto (1697–1768). Paul Getty Museum, Malibu.

Excavations in the Colosseum in a painting by H. Robert (1733–1808). Prado Museum, Madrid.

Colosseum, the arena seen from the north.

Colosseum, view of the cells beneath the arena.

13. THE VALLEY OF THE COLOSSEUM

Games in the Circus
and gladiators with
a bull, deer and ostrich
in mosaics in a villa
near Tusculum (fifth
century AD). Galleria
Borghese, Rome.

Gladiators
in a fourth-century
mosaic. Archaeological
Museum, Madrid.

were named according to their weapons. The *retiarius*, armed with net and trident, fought against the *mirmillo*, so called after the fish (*murma*) that decorated his helmet. Their combat symbolised the struggle between fisherman and fish. The "Samnites" were armed with a heavy sword and rectangular shield, while the "Thracians" fought with a short sword and small round shield. In provincial towns a vanquished combatant was rarely put to death: it took years to train a good gladiator and the impresario who mounted the games lost heavily by it. But in Rome, where the games were put on by the emperors, expense was no object and the public spared the losers only in exceptional circumstances.

Combats were also organised between criminals sentenced to death. In this case clemency was never shown: a swordsman who survived a series of gruelling combats would be dispatched by a fresh gladiator sent into the ring expressly for the purpose. Gladiatorial combats were not the only entertainment: there were also wild-animal hunts, fights between wild beasts, and even exhibitions of trained animals without bloodshed. The public reacted with admiration and excitement to the exotic animals and the unexpected appearance of the natural scenery and backdrops from which emerged fierce beasts and huntsmen.

THE ARCH OF CONSTANTINE

After defeating his rival Maxentius at the Battle of the Milvian Bridge (28 October 312) Constantine moved his residence to Trier in Germany. He only returned to Rome three years later to celebrate the tenth anniversary of his ascent to power. He inaugurated the arch that the Senate had erected in his honour on the long processional route followed by generals awarded a triumph. It ran from the Field of Mars through the city to the Temple of Capitoline Jove.

Since there was little time to complete the immense structure the Senate took the unprecedented step of scavenging parts of earlier monuments,

The Arch of Constantine, view of the south side.

Winged Victory,
relief from the reign
of Constantine.

Tondo from the reign
of Hadrian: hunting
scene.

especially public buildings from the reigns of Trajan, Hadrian and Marcus Aurelius. The four panels from the period of Trajan must originally have decorated the attic storey of the Basilica Ulpia, while the tondos from the period of Hadrian probably came from the entrance to a shrine dedicated to Antinous, Hadrian's young favourite. The carvings of Marcus Aurelius probably came from a triumphal arch celebrating his victories in Germany. For the sake of uniformity the faces of the emperors were all recarved to represent Constantine.

Carvings on the Arch of Constantine

"To the Emperor Caesar Flavius Constantinus Maximus Pius Felix Augustus, the Senate and People of Rome dedicated an arch decorated with scenes of triumph, since by divine inspiration and great wisdom with his army and righteous weapons he liberated the state from tyranny and all faction."
The inscription on the front of the arch represents Constantine as the restorer of the Empire, guided by divinity. The wars and triumphs of great emperors of the past cast and aura of legitimacy around his power and provided the political consensus needed for maintaining a stable government. The great storied frieze running along the middle of the smaller sides of the arch and above the lateral bays represents the Emperor's achievements: his departure from Milan; the siege of Verona, where he is crowned by a winged Victory; the defeat of Maxentius at the Milvian bridge; his entry into Rome; his speech to the population and a distribution of money. In the last two scenes Constantine appears in the middle of the composition, disproportionately larger than the other figures, ranged symmetrically on either side and facing him, clearly indicating their subordination.

THE DOMUS AUREA

Immediately after the fire of 64 AD, which destroyed most of the centre of Rome, Nero built a new imperial residence. This was far bigger and more luxurious than the previous one, the Domus Transitoria. Its walls were decked with gold and precious stones, giving it the name the Domus Aurea or Golden House. The new palace was immense: it covered the Palatine, Velia and Oppian hills and the valley where the Colosseum was later built. "Buildings the size of towns" surrounded a pool almost as big as a sea and behind them rose "villas with fields, vineyards and pastures, woods swarming with all sorts of creatures, wild and domestic." No less remarkable was the luxury of the ornaments, for we are told that "the dinning rooms had ceilings sheathed with movable plates of ivory and with apertures through which flowers and perfumes could be poured." Of the Domus Aurea there now remains a single pavilion on the Oppian, preserved because it was incorporated into the Baths of Trajan built over it. All memory of the palace was lost during the later Empire and Middle Ages. In the late fifteenth century it was rediscovered by artists and antiquarians, who would scramble into the underground grottoes filled with earth and there copy the decorations in the vaults. This gave rise to the new genre of decoration called "grotesque". After twenty years of continuous restoration work, which had to cope with some major problems, including the stability of the structures, today 32 of the finest chambers are open to the public. They include the nymphaeum of Ulysses and Polyphemus, the chamber of Achilles on Skyros, the chamber of Hector and Andromache, a hall with a gilded vault, and the monumental octagonal chamber. Visits are guided, with booking essential, for groups of 25 people. The temperature inside never rises above 12 °C degrees in summer and 4 °C in winter.

Scene at the centre of the vault in the Room of Achilles at Skyros.

Nero. Museo Palatino, Rome.

On the following pages Domus Aurea, octagonal room.

17. THE VALLEY OF THE COLOSSEUM

THE PALATINE
AND THE
CIRCUS
MAXIMUS

THE PALATINE AND THE CIRCUS MAXIMUS

2

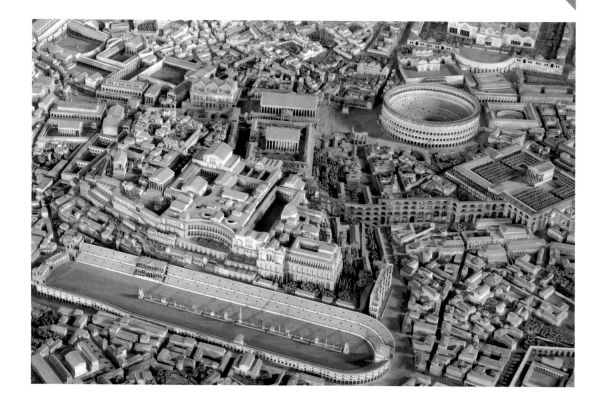

On the following pages
Ruins on the Palatine.

One of the nymphaeums
of the Domus Flavia.

Model of the central
archaeological area. Museo
della Civiltà Romana, Rome.

THE HISTORY OF PALATINE

According to Varro (116–27 BC), a celebrated scholar of Roman antiquities, Rome was founded on the Palatine in 754 BC by Romulus, who traced a furrow with a plough to mark its confines.

His account may be rather fanciful, but the Palatine was certainly the site of the earliest Latin settlement on the banks of the Tiber and also the nucleus of the Eternal City. Some very primitive religious traditions were connected with the Palatine.

One was the feast of the *Lupercalia*, connected with the she-wolf, Rome's sacred animal, when wolf-priests clothed in goatskins ran about the hill whipping all who chanced within reach. Throughout the republican period new cults were introduced to the Palatine and numerous temples erected.

The hill eventually became the residence of the Roman ruling class and it was here that Augustus was born. This was important for the hill's future because as emperor he fixed his residence on the hill and began to erect the Imperial Palaces on it.

In the following century an immense palace complex covered the Palatine, being frequently altered and extended till, by the end of the imperial period, it sprawled across the whole hill.

The Latin name of the hill, *Palatium*, became synonymous with the emperor's palace and with this meaning it eventually entered the various European languages.

The German poet Johann Wolfgang von Goethe (1749–1832) described the impressions aroused by the sight of the Palatine: "In the evening, after taking a leisurely view of all these beautiful things, we went to the Palatine gardens.

The spaces between the ruins and the imperial palaces have been made fertile and attractive by beds of flowers. We enjoyed a splendid evening congenial to our taste high up on an open terrace shaded by magnificent trees and surrounded by fragments of ornate capitals, smooth and fluted columns, shattered carvings and similar remains, as elsewhere there might be tables chairs and benches for some cheerful outdoor gathering. When, at the hour of sunset, we contemplated that rich and varied panorama with eyes wide-open and long practised, we had to confess that such a picture could still be admired even after all those that we had viewed during the day."

THE TEMPLE OF THE MAGNA MATER

The cult of Magna Mater (Great Mother) Cybele was introduced to Rome in 204 BC, during a difficult period of Roman history: for almost fifteen years the city had been engaged in warfare with the Carthaginian general Hannibal.

As part of the intense religious activity designed to curry favour with the gods, the Senate consulted the Sibylline books, a collection of prophecies, probably of Greek origin, traditionally believed to have been brought to Rome by Tarquin the Proud.

The simulacrum of the goddess, a black stone, perhaps a meteorite, shaped like an elongated cone, was removed from the sanctuary at Pessinus in

Two views of the Palatine at sunset.

Maidens carrying baskets by an incense brazier. Terracotta panel of the Augustan period from the Temple of Apollo Palatine. Museo Palatino, Rome.

Remains of the temple
of the Magna Mater.

The Magna Mater
enthroned, from
the Antonine period.
Museo Palatino, Rome.

25. THE PALATINE AND THE CIRCUS MAXIMUS

Asia Minor and brought to Rome, where it was kept in the Temple of Victory on the Palatine until a special shrine could be erected to the goddess. The Temple of the Magna Mater was inaugurated in 191 BC with the *Ludi Megalenses*, a series of spectacles with performances of works by Plautus and Terrence, written specially for the occasion.

The festival was repeated from 4–10 April every year to mark the arrival of the cult of Cybele in Rome.

THE HOUSE OF AUGUSTUS

Suetonius, a Roman historian and man of letters, has left a description of the house of Augustus on a site east of the Temple of the Magna Mater. "He moved to the Palatine, but again into a modest house that had belonged to Hortensius.

It was neither large nor luxurious. Outside it had only short porticoes with columns of Alban stone and the rooms were not floored with marble or mosaics of particular artistic value. For over forty years he slept, summer and winter, in the same bedroom."

Or returning to Rome in 36 BC, after defeating Sextus Pompey at Naulochos, Augustus bought up the adjoining buildings to create a complex consisting of his private home, which still stands, the Temple of Apollo and an official residence for public functions.

The residence was later incorporated into the palace of the Emperor Domitian, thereafter called the Domus Augustana.

THE TEMPLE OF APOLLO

In 36 BC Augustus started to build a temple dedicated to Apollo and completed it eight years later. It formed part of the public section of Augustus's residence, to which it was closely connected. The temple was built en-

The House of Livia
and the House of Augustus.

Statue of Augustus from
the Via Labicana. This portrait
depicts Augustus, perhaps
posthumously, as Pontifex
Maximus or High Priest,
a title he took in 12 BC.
Palazzo Massimo alle Terme,
Museo Nazionale Romano,
Rome.

Ruins of the Temple of Apollo.

Athene, Perseus and the
Gorgon in a terracotta panel
from the Augustan period
from the Temple of Apollo
Palatine. Museo Palatino,
Rome.

27. THE PALATINE AND THE CIRCUS MAXIMUS

tirely out of Luna marble (now called Carrara marble) and housed the cult statues of Apollo, Diana and Latona, the work of famous Greek sculptors four centuries earlier. The *Sibylline Books*, kept in golden caskets, were carefully stored in the base of the statue of Apollo.

The temple faced onto the Portico of the Danaides, so-called because it contained statues of the mythical daughters of King Danaus of Egypt. The temple may have been decorated with the splendid polychrome terracotta panels found on the site and now exhibited in the Museo Palatino. Of the whole complex today it is only possible to view the inner nucleus of the walls, stripped of its tuff cladding and with traces of marble floors and fragments of columns and capitals.

Fragment of wall decorations in the Domus Transitoria, mid-first century AD. Museo Palatino, Rome.

THE FRESCOES

Frescoes were the commonest form of wall decoration in ancient Rome. The colours were ground up in water and applied directly to the wet surface, usually several layers of plaster which were slow to dry and so enabled a large area to be covered with paintings.

The Room of Masks in the House of Augustus has a fairly complex decorative scheme. In what is known as the "second Pompeian style," the walls seem to open out into *trompe l'oeil* vistas between architectural motifs typical of stage painting.

The theatrical theme is continued in the masks decorating the cornices painted on the walls. In the middle of each wall appears a painting of a rural shrine.

This seems to be the bedroom where Augustus slept for over forty years, while the adjoining room, decorated with festoons of pine fronds between slender pillars, may be the Empress Livia's bedroom. The frescoes of the room known as the Aula Isiaca represent a late phase of the "second Pompeian style."

Frescoes in the Aula
Isiaca, 30–20 BC.

Room of the Masks
in the House of Augustus.

They exemplify the fashion for Egyptian art which influenced Roman painting between the period when Caesar brought Cleopatra to Rome and the
aftermath of the battle of Actium (31 BC), culminating in the death of the
celebrated queen.

The paintings from a room below the basilica of the Domus Flavia, now in
a Renaissance loggia close by the Museo Palatino depict myths of the
Egyptian goddess Isis and her cult symbols. The whole of the pictorial
decoration of the Aula Isiaca, now partly lost but reconstructed from drawings and watercolours made by eighteenth-century artists when the room
was rediscovered, is a clear profession of faith in the Egyptian deities. The
richness and refinement of the frescoes and stuccos, enhanced by gener-
ous gilding, show this chamber was part of a rich and imposing Palatine
dwelling.

Splendid frescoes also come from the Domus Transitoria was Nero's first
home. It linked the buildings erected on the Palatine by his predecessors
with the imperial buildings on the Esquiline.

Only a few chambers and some of the decorations still survive: the rest was
burned down in the terrible fire which destroyed half the buildings of Rome
on the night of 19 July, 64 AD.

THE DOMUS TIBERIANA

The complex built by Tiberius on the Palatine covered much of the west
side of the hill between the Temple of the Great Mother and the hillside
towards the forum, perhaps the site of the emperor's paternal home. The
buildings are little known, as the area was covered in the sixteenth century by the garden of the Farnese family, part of which still exists, so that
excavations have only explored the margins of the buildings.

We know that the residence of Tiberius was enlarged by Caligula and restored by Domitian, Hadrian and Septimius Severus. It long remained in

The Domus Tiberiana.

Sardonyx cameo with
the bust of Tiberius
from the first half
of the first century AD.
Kunsthistorisches
Museum, Vienna.

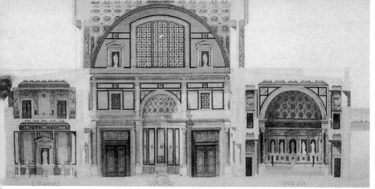

The Domus Flavia (conjectural reconstruction and present state).

Section through the Domus Flavia (conjectural) in a watercolour by F. Dutert (1845-1905).

Domitian (81–96 AD). Musei Capitolini, Rome.

use as the residence of the designated heir to the empire, while the reigning emperor occupied the nearby Domus Augustana. For example Marcus Aurelius and Lucius Verus both moved here after their adoption by the Emperor Antoninus Pius.

THE DOMUS FLAVIA

The Emperor Domitian, like his predecessors, established his residence and court on the Palatine. The great palace, inaugurated in 92 AD, had two entrances, one to the state rooms (the Domus Flavia) and one to the private apartments (the Domus Augustana, p. 34).

The official part of the building was laid out around a large porticoed court with various reception rooms ranged round it. In particular a splendid state room, called the Aula Regia, decorated with niches set between columns, served as the audience chamber. Here the throne was placed in the middle of an apse.

At the side of the throne room there was a basilica, its interior divided in three by two rows of columns, and a building (the *lararium*), where images of members of the royal family were placed after their deaths. On the opposite side of the courtyard stood the great triclinium or banqueting hall flanked by two smaller rooms at the centre of which were two oval fountains (nymphaeums).

The playing of the waters could be admired by the banqueters through the great windows between the triclinium and the side chambers. Hadrian installed a heating system in the banqueting hall so that it could be used in winter.

31. THE PALATINE AND THE CIRCUS MAXIMUS

The marble pavement still visible was part of restoration work under Maxentius.

Domitian's palace aroused the admiration of his contemporaries by its splendour and the immense size of the lofty chambers, probably decorated with marble and richly furnished.

The grandeur of the architecture and the natural setting of the palace created the impression that it was truly the dwelling of a *dominus et deus*, a god reigning on earth.

THE DOMUS AUGUSTANA

The private wing of the Palace of Domitian was called the Domus Augustana because it incorporated Augustus's official residence. It was built on two levels to match the slope of the Palatine Hill. Its curving facade with the main entrance faced the Circus Maximus. On entering from this side, one passed through the outer chambers and came to an inner court surrounded by columns (called a peristyle). This was largely occupied by a monumental fountain decorated with a pattern formed by four *peltae*, shields shaped like half-moons legendarily used by the Amazons.

Around this courtyard were ranged symmetrically the rooms of the house of Domitian, laid out on two floors and with vaulted ceilings. A staircase led to the upper floor, the official residence, where a second peristyle was decorated with a large pool with a little island in the middle, on which stood a temple, perhaps to Minerva.

The emperor probably only occupied the rooms on the upper floor, recognisable by their complex layout and small size.

Peristyle of the Domus Augustana.

Dancer from the age of Hadrian in the Domus Augustiana. Museo Palatino, Rome.

View of the Domus Augustana.

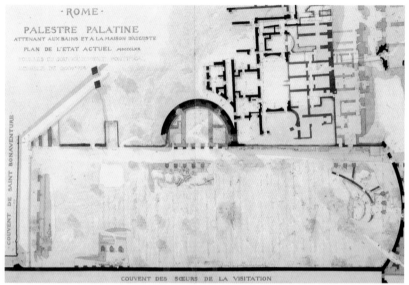

Plan of the Palatine Stadium, drawing by J.L. Pascal (1837–1920). Ecole des Beaux-Arts, Paris.

Conjectural reconstruction of the Palatine Stadium, watercolour by J.L. Pascal (1837–1920). Ecole des Beaux-Arts, Paris.

Aphrodite, from the reign of Pius Antoninus, from the Palatine Stadium. Museo Palatino, Rome.

THE STADIUM

Domitian's private residence was connected with an enormous garden in the form of stadium, 160 metres long, used for chariot racing. Decorated by fountains, its perimeter was bounded by a two-storey portico. A spine ran down the middle of the stadium and formed the longitudinal axis around which the chariots raced.

At one end an imposing stand enabled the emperor to watch the races in the Circus Maximus without leaving his palace. A little more than a century after construction of the Domus Augustana, the Emperor Septimius Severus ordered his baths to be built next to the Stadium as part of a vast program of architectural improvement of the slopes of the Palatine. They were set above massive vaults and their façade formed a monumental fountain called the *Septizodium*. The great arches of the baths are still clearly visible from the valley of the Circus Maximus.

THE MUSEO PALATINO

The earliest antiquarian museum of the Palatine was opened in the Domus Tiberiana in the later nineteenth century. On display were items discovered in excavations organised by the French Emperor Napoleon III. Then in 1882 the government ordered that "all the objects contained in the Museo Pala-

The Palatine Stadium.

The baths of Septimius Severus.

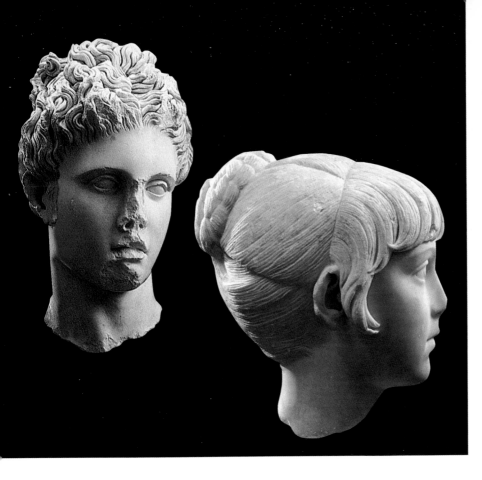

Marble head of Apollo from excavations of the Domus Augustiana, dating from between the late Flavian period and the mid-second century AD. Museo Palatino, Rome.

This elegantly coiffured young woman has been identified as one of the daughters of the Emperor Marcus Aurelius and his wife Faustina. Museo Palatino, Rome.

An ephebe carved in basalt from the Augustan period found near the Temple of Apollo. Museo Palatino, Rome.

tino should be moved as soon as possible to Santa Maria degli Angeli alle Terme". Since then all the most important items found on the Palatine have been added to the collections of the Museo delle Terme. At the beginning of the twentieth century there was already a widely felt need for an independent museum on the Palatine.

Yet, despite the objections of some scholars, all finds of artistic interest continued to be sent to the Museo delle Terme, while the Antiquario del Palatino was used for less valuable exhibits closely connected with the site and the palace.

The Museo Palatino occupies a former convent built on top of Domitian's Palace. Its present display is part of a broad plan for reorganising the various branches of the Museo Nazionale Romano. Apart from a section dedicated to Rome in the archaic period, the museum has displays of art in the imperial palaces from Augustus to late imperial times.

THE CIRCUS MAXIMUS

Erected in the valley between the Palatine and Aventine hills, the Circus Maximus was 600 metres long and up to 200 metres wide, with a spine that must have been 340 metres long. It could hold 200,000 spectators, making it one of the biggest buildings for public spectacles of all time. The earliest installations were the work of Tarquin Priscus (seventh-sixth centuries BC), but construction proper only began in 329 BC, with the erection of the starting gates for the chariots and the central spine.

In 174 BC the seven "eggs" were placed on the spine to mark to number of circuits of the course.

In 33 BC Agrippa added seven bronze dolphins. Augustus's principal addition was the obelisk of the Pharoah Ramses II (thirteenth century BC), brought from Heliopolis and erected on the spine. Much later, in 357 AD, Constantius II added a second obelisk, that of Thothmes III (fifteenth cen-

Reconstruction of a hut
erected on the Palatine
in the eighth century BC.
Museo Palatino, Rome.

Probably from the Temple
of Apollo is the fresco
of Apollo crowned with
a laurel wreath from
the Augustan period.
Museo Palatino, Rome.

On the following pages
View of the Circus Maximus
from inside the arena
towards the Tiber.

tury BC) from Thebes. In 1587 both of the shattered obelisks were unearthed by Pope Sixtus V. The first was later placed in Piazza del Popolo and the second in Piazza di San Giovanni in Laterano.

The circus remained in use throughout late antiquity. The last races were held there in 549 AD by Totila, king of the Ostrogoths.

Races at the Circus

The race-track in the circus was divided down the middle by a masonry spine with a pillar (*meta*) at each end to mark the turns. The chariots, drawn by two or four horses, were extremely light and it took great skill on the part of the charioteers to keep them from overturning (though disastrous falls were one of the attractions for spectators). The skill of the charioteer lay in turning the chariot as sharply as possible so as to gain ground. The rules allowed all sorts of foul play to obstruct opponents and send them crashing into the walls.

Horses and chariots were divided into teams, distinguished by different colours, and each had its supporters: the various colours eventually formed factions and strongly influenced political life.

The charioteers were idolised and if particularly skilful might accumulate immense fortunes.

One Diocles, of Portuguese origin, raced for the Reds for twenty-four years in the second century AD. He won 3,000 times with a two-horse chariot and 1462 times with a four-horse team. When he retired he had accumulated the fabulous sum of 35 million sesterces.

Around the circuses, like football stadiums today, there stood myriads of taverns, kiosks, and booths. While the spectators on the terraces watched up to a hundred races a day, thieves, prostitutes, peddlers and hucksters of all sorts mingled with the crowd.

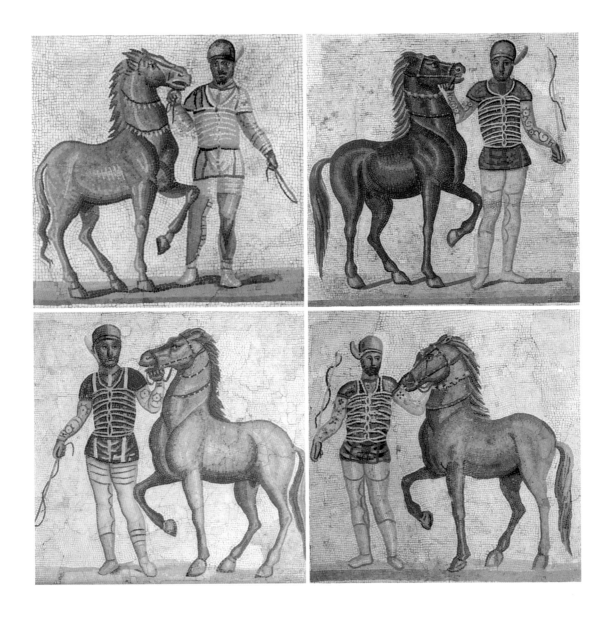

41. THE PALATINE AND THE CIRCUS MAXIMUS

THE ROMAN FORUM

THE ROMAN FORUM

**On the previous pages
Overall view of the Forum.**

**The Column of Foca
and the Arch of Septimius
Severus. In the background
the church of Saints Luca
and Martina, 1635–1664.**

View of the Forum at night.

HISTORY

The depression occupied by the Forum, between the Palatine and the Capitol, was originally a marshy area watered by the Velabrum, a stream that flowed into the Tiber and made the whole area unhealthy. In about the seventh century BC the Velabrum was channelled into the Cloaca Maxima, a canal that drained the north-east part of Rome.

The Roman Forum soon became the centre of civic life. The area was progressively occupied by religious, political and commercial buildings and then commemorative monuments.

The original dirt surface was eventually paved and this paving was relaid several times over the centuries. The existing pavement was laid in 9 BC by order of the praetor L. Naevius Surdinus after a series of fires had destroyed much of the Forum.

For over a thousand years the Forum remained the focus of civic life and new buildings continued to be erected. Then, in the Middle Ages, it was completely forgotten and reduced to a meadow called the Campo Vaccino ("cow pasture").

The most disastrous period of its existence was the Renaissance. Pope Julius II (1503-1513), planning to rebuild Rome, pillaged the area for building materials

and ancient marbles were often ground up for the lime-kiln. According to
eye-witnesses like Pirro Ligorio the destruction of ancient monuments
continued apace: at times a whole building, almost perfectly preserved,
would be demolished in a month, despite the protests of Raphael or the
misgivings of Michelangelo.

When the spoliation was complete the area reverted to cow pasture until
the nineteenth century, when the Forum was carefully explored by the first
archaeologists of modern times.

THE BASILICAS

Normally the legal, political, and commercial business of the forum was
conducted out of doors, but in bad weather it was moved into great roofed
halls called basilicas.

Two rows of regular columns divided the interiors into a nave and two side
aisles. The nave would be built higher so that windows could be set in its
sides to light the interior.

The only basilica to survive from the republican period is the Basilica Ful-
via Aemilia erected in 179 BC by the censors Marcus Aemilius Lepidus and
Marcus Fulvius Nobilior. Its present form is the result of extensive restoration in the imperial period.

The construction of the Basilica Julia between the two main streets from
the Tiber to the Forum–the *Vicus Iugarius* and the *Vicus Tuscus*–probably

48. THE ROMAN FORUM

entailed their deviation and the relaying of the road surface. The building, which was commissioned by Julius Caesar in 54 BC, was completed nearly fifty years later under Augustus. Its present appearance is the result of restoration under Diocletian.

THE CURIA

The Curia Hostilia, the Roman Senate's most ancient meeting-place, probably stood on the present site of the church of Santi Luca and Martina. The great brick edifice now called the Curia was the new Senate House, begun by order of Julius Caesar and completed by Augustus in 29 BC. In the seventh century it was turned into a church and this saved it from destruction. In the 1930s it was restored to the state in which it was left after being rebuilt by the Emperor Diocletian.

The interior of the curia is a single large space covering an area of almost 500 square metres. The ceiling is 21 metres high. Much of the intarsia marble pavement still dates from the age of Diocletian, as do the architectural decorations on the walls.

The three steps that run round the longer sides once supported the seats of the senators (numbering about three hundred), while at the far end is the dais for the president. The bronze doors are a copy of those dating from the time of Diocletian. In the seventeenth century the originals were moved to the basilica of San Giovanni in Laterano, where they can still be seen in the central portal.

THE WEST SIDE

The west side of the Forum is dominated by remains of the imposing colonnades of the portico of the *Dii Consentes* (the counselling deities), and the temples of Vespasian, Titus, and Saturn.

The original plan of the Temple of Saturn dates from the fifth century BC; it survives now in a reconstruction from the third century AD. In 303 AD, to commemorate the twentieth year of the rule of Diocletian and Maximian and the tenth year of government by Galerius and Constantius Chlorus, a monument was erected of which only the base of a column now survives: originally it must have supported a statue of Constantius Chlorus. The base, known as the "base of the Decennials", is decorated by two great figures of Victory and scenes of sacrifice in which the emperor himself takes part, assisted by various deities, including Mars and the goddess Roma.

In 608, Smaragdus, the hexarch of Italy, dedicated a celebratory monument to the Emperor Phocas: according to the inscription on the base it was a column surmounted by a golden statue. The column and its Corinthian capital are still visible not far from the Temple of Saturn. Probably taken from a building of the third century AD, it was the last monument to be erected in the Forum. In the travertine pavement immediately to the east of the column of Phocas can be seen a bronze inscription commemorating the re-paving of the Forum under Augustus by command of the urban praetor L. Naevius Surdinus. The inscription was restored in 1955.

The Temple of Saturn and, left, the Temple of Vespasian and Titus.

Detail of the base of the Decennials: procession of senators.

Remains of the west side of the Forum and a conjectural reconstruction of the monumental complex in a watercolour by C. Mayo (1835–1911). Ecole des Beaux-Arts, Paris.

THE ARCH OF SEPTIMIUS SEVERUS

In 203 AD the Senate erected a great arch with three bays (called *fornices*) to commemorate the victories of Septimius Severus against the Parthians, a people of Asia Minor. This triple-vaulted monument was erected just where the Via Sacra begins to climb toward the Capitol, the culminating point of triumphal processions awarded to victorious generals. The arch is wholly sheathed in marble and an image on a coin shows it was originally surmounted by bronze sculptures: a chariot drawn by six horses flanked with equestrian statues symbolising the triumph decreed to the emperor. In the carvings on the arch the same theme is expressed in the small frieze above the two lesser vaults. This shows carts filled with booty, soldiers, prisoners, and the great statue of a seated figure personifying the conquered province. On the attic is carved the dedication: in the fourth line the name of Septimius Severus's younger son Geta was effaced by order of his brother Caracalla, who had him put to death and decreed the oblivion of his memory (*damnatio memoriae*).

THE TEMPLE OF ANTONINUS AND FAUSTINA

The great temple above which the church of San Lorenzo in Miranda was built in the seventh and eighth centuries has been identified with a fair degree of certainty from the dedicatory inscription still legible on the architrave. The temple was erected in 141 AD in honour and memory of Faustina, the wife of Antoninus Pius, deified after her death. Twenty years later, on the death of the emperor, the first line was added to the inscription, so that the temple was rededicated to both the deified spouses. The building stands on a tall plinth preceded by a flight of brick steps, rebuilt in

Arch of Septimius Severus.

Temple of Antoninus and Faustina.

The Basilica of Maxentius.

modern times, which has incorporated the ancient core, also made of brick. Like other monuments in the Forum, the Temple of Antoninus and Faustina risked being dismantled in the sixteenth century when the marble slabs with which it was sheathed were removed. The workmen, however, were unable to remove the columns. Still visible at their tops are the deep grooves scored in the tops of the shafts by ropes used in the attempt to topple them. The flower beds of different shapes and sizes to the east of the temple reproduce the forms of the tombs of the archaic burial place (Bronze Age, tenth–eighth centuries BC) discovered early last century.

THE BASILICA OF MAXENTIUS

Built in the early fourth century on the site of the earlier *Horrea Piperataria*, warehouses for pepper and spices, the basilica was completed by Constantine, who also had to alter its design. The basilica covers 6500 square meters and is divided into a large nave with side aisles. The ceiling of the nave consists of three immense cross-vaults resting on eight columns 14.5 metres tall. The last surviving column was removed by Pope Paul V to Piazza Santa Maria Maggiore, where it stands today. The side aisles have coffered barrel vaults.

In the west apse there was a colossal statue erected by Maxentius and after his death resculpted to represent Constantine. It was an acrolith, i.e. a statue with the head, arms and legs of marble and the rest of the body of

Atrium of the House
of the Vestal Virgins.

Remains of the Temple
of Vesta.

some other material, in this case probably gilded bronze. The marble parts, brought to light in 1487, are now in the Musei Capitolini.

THE TEMPLE OF VESTA AND THE HOUSE OF THE VESTALS

Vesta was the goddess of the hearth and her worship was overseen by six priestesses from the patrician families of Rome. Chosen in childhood, between the ages of six and ten, they had to serve the goddess as virgins for at least thirty years.

The priestesses enjoyed many privileges, but those that broke their vows were condemned to the cruel punishment of being buried alive.

At the end of their priesthood they were allowed to marry. Very few of them ever did so, as it was held to be ill-fated.

The temple of Vesta, a round edifice with a hole in the centre of its conical roof, preserved the sacred fire. One result of this was that it tended to burn down frequently. It was rebuilt several times, in different materials, until it was restructured in the late second century by Julia Domna, the wife of Septimius Severus. Next to it stood the dwelling of the priestesses, laid out around a courtyard with porticoes running round the four sides and fountains and pools in the middle. Here must have stood the numerous statues of the Vestal Virgins revealed in excavations. The priestesses lived in comfortable rooms heated with stoves on the upper floor and had numerous warm baths for their use.

THE ARCH OF TITUS

The arch was erected by the Senate and people of Rome in memory of the Emperor Titus. The monument, not mentioned by ancient writers, can be identified by the dedicatory inscription still legible on the side toward the Colosseum.

The monument has a single archway (fornix) and a small frieze running round the four sides above the architrave. It represents Vespasian and Titus's triumph over the Jews in 71 AD after the destruction of Jerusalem. The carved panel on the south side within the arch depicts soldiers bearing away the plunder from the temple of Jerusalem: they include the silver trumpets and seven-branched candelabrum, of which this is the earliest depiction.

In the Middle Ages the arch, like the Colosseum, was incorporated into the fortress of the Frangipane family and so survived. As can be seen in the inscription facing the Forum, in 1882 Pope Pius VII commissioned the architect Giuseppe Valadier to restore the pillars damaged by the creation of a little room inside the archway.

THE TEMPLE OF VENUS AND ROMA

The most important temple in Rome was designed by Hadrian. Begun in 121 AD, it was completed by his successor Antoninus Pius.
In his design, Hadrian demolished the portico, modifying all that remained of the monumental entrance to the Domus Aurea.

Vestal in the atrium of the House of the Vestal.

The Arch of Titus.

Arch of Titus in a painting by A.L.R. Ducros (1748–1810). Musée Cantonal des Beaux-Arts, Lausanne.

Onyx cameo with the bust of Titus (79–81 AD). Museo Archeologico Nazionale, Florence.

57. THE ROMAN FORUM

He used twenty-four elephants to move the Colossus of Nero from its original position, altered the head and turned it into a representation of the Sun.

Finally he artificially enlarged the summit of the Velia to create a platform capable of accommodating the building.

The temple, surrounded by a colonnaded portico, had two main chambers (*cellae*) facing in opposite directions: they housed the cult statues of Roma on the side toward the Forum) and Venus (the side toward the Colosseum). Hadrian's plan, based on Greek models, brought him into conflict with Trajan's architect, Apollodorus of Damascus, who outspokenly criticised the lack of a tall plinth to support the building and the disproportion between the size of the statue and that of the *cella*. Cassius Dio reports that he commented, "'If the gods wanted to stand up and walk out they could not.' This sharp written comment angered and troubled Hadrian who felt he had committed an irremediable error." Apollodorus was put to death by the emperor for his outspokenness.

59. THE ROMAN FORUM

THE IMPERIAL
FORUMS

On the previous pages
The Markets and the Forum
of Trajan.

Trajan's Column.

Trajan's Column, detail.

The Julian Forum.

HISTORY

When the republic came to an end the Roman Forum seemed absolutely inadequate for the functions of administration and display required of a city that was the capital of an empire extending from Gaul (modern France) to Syria.

Consequently Julius Caesar started to build a new monumental complex, which at first appeared merely the extension of the original Forum, though it also involved some radical changes.

In the course of the next hundred and fifty years and the reigns of many emperors a new architectural complex grew up round the Imperial Forums to house the centre of government.

The new development covered about nine hectares of land, mostly privately owned and already covered with buildings which had to be purchased and demolished.

Clearly the cost of the operation, though phased over a long time span, must have been astronomic.

The Imperial Forums, for centuries the centre of the city's life, were the preferred spot for displaying statues and inscriptions to the great men and women of Rome and victorious generals.

Their principal function, however, was to provide adequate space for the public and religious ceremonies by

which the Roman state displayed itself in all its majesty to its citizens and subjects.

THE JULIAN FORUM

In 54 BC, on Caesar's behalf, Cicero purchased the land necessary for construction of a new forum. It was 160 metres long and 75 wide, surrounded on three sides by a double colonnade and closed on the west side by the Temple of Venus Genetrix. In the middle of the square stood an equestrian statue of Caesar (actually an existing statue of Alexander with the head resculpted).
Construction of the forum was a lengthy process and was only completed after Caesar's death. In 46 BC Octavian inaugurated the temple dedicated to Venus, the mythical founder of the Gens Iulia, or Julian clan, in fulfilment of a vow by Caesar before the decisive battle against Pompey at Pharsalia (48 BC).

THE FORUM OF NERVA

Construction of the Forum of Nerva was decided by Domitian to give monumental form to the vacant strip of land at the point where the two existing forums met.
The emperor died shortly before the work was completed and it was finished by Nerva, at the time aged sixty-six, who gave it his name.
The new forum, 120 metres long and 45 wide, allowed no space for the construction of a new colonnade, so the portico of the Temple of Peace was

65. THE IMPERIAL FORUMS

used. At one end a temple was dedicated to Minerva: this stood till 1606 when Pope Paul V had it pulled down to provide materials for the construction of the Acqua Paola on the Janiculum.

THE FORUM OF AUGUSTUS

The construction of the Forum of Augustus, with surface area of over a hectare, was the result of a vow made by Octavian, later the Emperor Augustus, before the battle of Philippi against Caesar's assassins (42 BC). Its significance is expressed by the temple to Mars Ultor (the Avenger) that dominates its north side.

Work on the new forum went on for almost forty years and it was inaugurated in 2 BC.

The function of this monumental area was to provide greater space for the crowd than the Roman Forum and Caesar's Forum. But it became above all a centre of display designed to glorify the emperor, who is represented on a majestic triumphal chariot in the middle of the square.

The Forum of Augustus had a distinctively military character: it was here that the senate would meet to declare war or peace and here were erected the statues of victorious generals, now they were no longer awarded a triumph, as this had become the exclusive privilege of the emperors.

THE FORUM OF TRAJAN

This forum was built by the Emperor Trajan between 107 and 113 AD. It was financed by the immense wealth from the conquest of Dacia and the work was overseen by the most famous architect of the day, Apollodorus of Damascus.

Since the space between the existing forum and the hillsides was already taken up by buildings, Apollodorus had to cut into the ridge between the

The Forum of Nerva.

Architectural details of the forum of Augustus.

Augustus, copy of a bronze original (20 BC) commissioned by Livia after his death for her villa at Prima Porta. Rome, Musei Vaticani.

The Forum of Augustus.

The Basilica Ulpia.

Views of the Markets of Trajan.

Quirinal and the Capitol. The new complex was truly immense (300 x 85 metres).

The Forum proper was entered through a monumental arch with a single vault.

The two longer sides were colonnaded and in the middle stood an imposing equestrian statue of Trajan.

A large part of Trajan's Forum and Markets were brought to light by urban clearances during the Fascist period, but only the excavations conducted in the last fifteen years have made it possible to bring to reveal 15000 square metres of the Forum and reconstruct the urban history of the site from the republican period down to the Middle Ages.

Thanks to a complex museological project, many fragments of architecture and sculpture from the buildings in the Forum are now on display in the interiors of Trajan's Markets.

Against the background of the forum rise the remains of the Basilica Ulpia, which contained important state archives and two libraries designed by Apollodorus, one utilised to store records in Latin and the other for those in Greek, a reflection of the empire's bilingualism.

The books, both rolls and bound codices, were kept in wooden presses set in the recesses still visible in the walls.

The books were carefully catalogued and looked after by librarians, whose tasks included protecting them from damp.

Views of the Markets of Trajan.

Trajan (98–117 AD), Archaeological Museum, Ankara.

69. THE IMPERIAL FORUMS

THE MARKETS OF TRAJAN

The Markets of Trajan.

After excavating the hillside to build the Forum of Trajan, the slopes of the Quirinal were shored up by a complex of brick buildings known as the Markets of Trajan. Their facade consisted of a great exedra with semi-circular chambers at either end, perhaps used as schools or auditoria. There is reliable evidence that at least in late imperial times the forum was used for courses of higher studies with access to the two libraries nearby.

The middle of the complex housed shops (*tabernae*): eleven on the ground floor and ten on the first floor, facing a passageway. The shops on the upper floor, however, faced in the opposite direction and opened onto a street behind, Via Biberatica. The name, recorded only in the Middle Ages, was derived from the Latin noun *biber* (drink) and probably indicates that some of the shops were taverns and sold refreshments.

The Markets of Trajan were also occupied by retailers, but their principal use must have been as wholesale warehouses dealing in provisions and run by the state. They thus formed the last link in a chain of distribution that also included Trajan's important new port at Fiumicino.

TRAJAN'S COLUMN

The column erected by Trajan between the two libraries in his forum is made up of nineteen cylindrical blocks of marble. Set on a pedestal and topped by a great capital, the column measures 29.78 metres or one hundred Roman feet: a carefully calculated height. The shaft of the column once sup-

Detail of carvings
on Trajan's Column.

Trajan's Column in the
Napoleonic period.
Anonymous watercolour
of the nineteenth century.
Biblioteca dell'Istituto
di Storia dell'Arte, Rome.

On the following pages
Anonymous (sixteenth
century), drawings of the
reliefs on Trajan's Column,
details. Two embassies
of Dacians before Trajan;
Dacian cavalry drowned
in midstream; sacrifice
in camp; Trajan
with a group of women
prisoners; Dacians fleeing
into a forest pursued
by Numidian cavalry;
sacrifice before the great
bridge on the Danube.
Private collection.

ported a statue of Trajan that disappeared in the Middle Ages and was
replaced by one of St. Peter in the sixteenth century. It rests on a cube-shaped
plinth decorated with trophies and shields carved in very low relief. A door
is set in the base with an inscription above it stating that the purpose of
the monument was to indicate the original height of the hill excavated to
construct the Forum of Trajan.
On the emperor's death his ashes were placed on a marble ledge inside a
chamber occupying the whole north side of the base. This function was
envisaged when the column was built, confirming that it must have been
designed as Trajan's funerary monument.

Carvings on the Column

The decoration of Trajan's column is without precedent. It is a continuous
carved frieze about 200 metres long, originally painted, which unfolds in a
spiral around the shaft of the column.
It illustrates episodes of the two wars waged and won by Trajan against the
Dacians in 101–102 and 105–106 AD. The scenes from the two campaigns
are separated by the figure of Victory writing on a shield.
The artist's intention was to provide a faithful record of events as they
actually occurred. Given the column's position between the two libraries
and the form of the carvings, it is likely that it was a reproduction of an
ancient book in roll form and the carvings were a figurative representation
of Trajan's *Commentaries*, now lost, written in Dacia.
The frieze depicts minutely the main episodes of the war, though they repeat
the same sequence of incidents: from the start of the campaign with the
crossing of the Danube by a bridge of boats to the deportation of the vanquished population, with battles, sieges, the construction of camps, speech-
es to the troops, and executions. The figure of Trajan appears no fewer than
sixty times.

74. THE IMPERIAL FORUMS

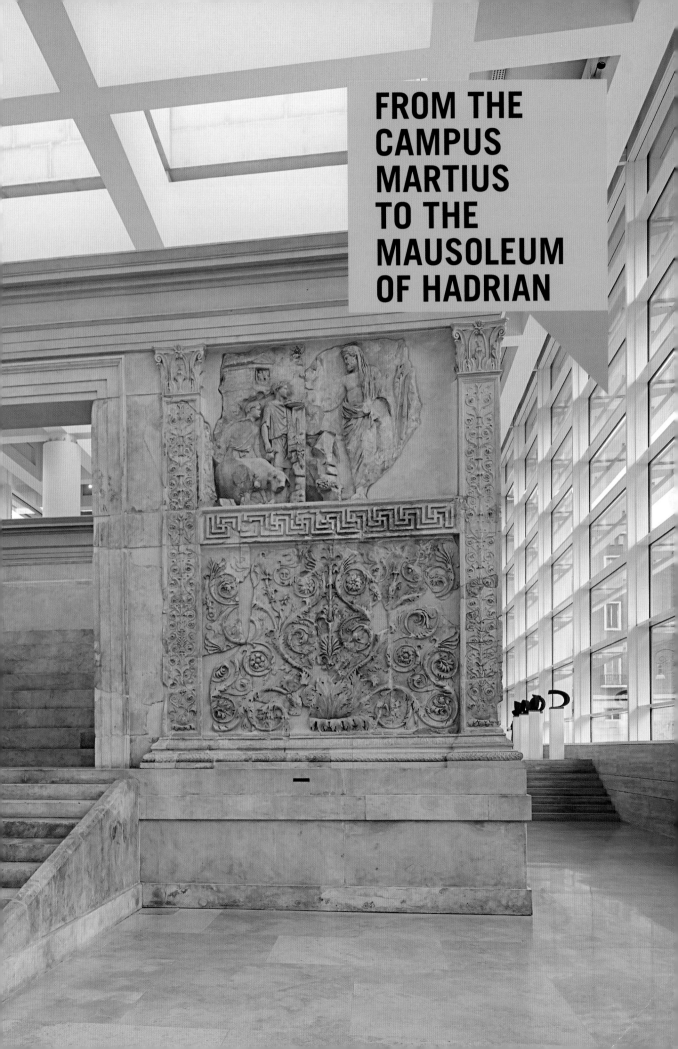

FROM THE
CAMPUS
MARTIUS
TO THE
MAUSOLEUM
OF HADRIAN

IL CAMPO
MARZIO
DELL'ANTICA ROMA
OPERA
DI·G·B·PIRANESI
SOCIO DELLA·REAL·SOCIETÀ
DEGLI ANTIQVARI DI LONDRA

On the previous pages
The Ara Pacis.

Imaginary reconstruction
of the Campus Martius
in a drawing by G.B. Piranesi
(1720-1778).

Theatre of Marcellus, side
facing the Forum Holitorium.

THE CAMPUS MARTIUS IN HISTORY

The Campus Martius or Field of Mars is an area of flood-plain lying in the great bend of the Tiber and stretching as far as the slopes of the Pincius, the Quirinal and the Capitol. It was originally a pasture lying outside the city's religious boundary (called the *pomerium*) within which it was forbidden to bear arms. For this reason it was free from buildings–though they gradually encroached–and used for military reviews and exercises. The middle of the Campus Martius was occupied by the *Saepta*, a large rectangular space covering over 10,000 square metres. The *comitia tributa*, assemblies of the common people, were held here.

The construction of monumental urban architecture on the Campus Martius began under the republic, in the second century BC, and culminated in a grand project conceived by Julius Caesar. He erected numerous buildings and the future Theatre of Marcellus and also planned to deviate the course of the Tiber to unite the Campus Martius with the Vatican hill.

Caesar's death prevented execution of the plan. In the reign of Augustus the layout of the area was further altered, largely under the influence of Agrippa.

A new and intense phase of construction began after the fire of 80 AD that devastated the whole of the Cam-

The Theatre of Marcellus
in a drawing by G.B. Piranesi
(1720–1778).

East side of the Theatre
of Marcellus.

pus Martius. In the second century AD the central part of the plain was used mainly for funerals of the emperors and their apotheosis (deification of the dead ruler by his successor or the Senate), as is shown, for example, by the Column of Antoninus.

The Campus Martius was traversed by the Via Lata, the urban stretch of the Via Flaminia, whose route matches the present Via del Corso. It continued to be inhabited throughout the Middle Ages and still preserves the ancient street layout and the principal blocks of buildings.

THE THEATRE OF MARCELLUS

The new theatre was erected on a site before the Temple of Apollo Sosianus, probably the same spot where, in the republican period, there used to be a temporary theatre. Its construction was begun by Caesar but he probably had time to do little more than clear the site by demolishing part of the Circus Flaminius.

The building was completed by Augustus, who in 13 or 11 BC dedicated it to his nephew Marcellus, his designated heir who had died prematurely ten years earlier.

The theatre was over 32 metres high and its cavea (auditorium) had a diameter of 130 metres and held over 15,000 spectators.

During the Middle Ages the building was occupied by the Savelli family and in the eighteenth century by the Orsini. The upper part of the cavea, preserved to a height of 20 metres, is now incorporated into a mansion designed at the start of the sixteenth century by Baldassarre Peruzzi. Its present appearance and isolation from the buildings round it are the result of demolition work in 1926–1932.

THE THEATRE AND CURIA OF POMPEY

Construction of the complex began in 61 BC, after Pompey's triple triumph and continued for five years. The porticoes, once decorated with statues, have not survived; the only remains are some relics of the great rectangular exedra which opened out in front of the theatre and was used for meetings of the senate.

Here, at the foot of Pompey's statue, Caesar was assassinated on 15 March, 44 BC. Far better preserved is the theatre itself: its inner curve is repeated in the elevation of the apartment block on Via di Grotta Pinta. The inauguration of the theatre, which could hold over 17,000 people, was celebrated with sumptuous entertainments.

THE TEMPLES OF APOLLO SOSIANUS AND BELLONA

Following a plague epidemic, in 431 BC a temple was dedicated to Apollo the Healer on the site of an earlier shrine to the same deity. It was repaired and refurbished on various occasions, then in 34 BC wholly rebuilt, probably by Gaius Sosius, slightly set back from its previous position. The new temple was richly decorated and had a marble floor. The pediment depicted a battle with Amazons before the goddess Athene: these carvings date from the fifth century BC and were taken from a Greek temple. The interior of the cell was like a museum, being filled with classical Greek paintings and sculpture.

East of the temple can be seen the remains of the Temple of Bellona, built by Appius Claudius Caecus after 296 BC. Sessions of the Senate were frequently held in these temples, especially when decreeing a triumph.

Building that repeats the structure of the Theatre of Pompey in Via di Grotta Pinta.

On the following pages The Theatre of Marcellus and the Temple of Apollo Sosianus.

THE PORTICO OF OCTAVIA

The north side of the Circus Flaminius, erected in 221 BC
and now demolished, was bounded by a number of great
porticoes.

The only one to survive is the Portico of Octavia: originally
erected in 146 BC by the future consul Quintus Caecilius
Metellus Macedonicus, it was rebuilt in the Augustan period. During its reconstruction between 33 and 23 BC–for-
mally attributed to Augustus's sister Octavia–the portico
was enlarged to its present dimensions by incorporating
the Curia and library of Octavia.

Among the works of art that decorated the portico there
was the statue of Cornelia, the mother of the Gracchi (the
first likeness of a woman to be exhibited publicly at Rome,
in around 100 BC).

There were also thirty-four equestrian statues by the Greek
sculptor Lysippus, taken by Metellus from the shrine of

The Portico of Octavia.

The Portico
of Octavia, drawing
by G.B. Piranesi
(1720–1778).

Dion in Macedonia. They portrayed Alexander the Great and those of his
cavalry who died at the battle of the Granicus.

**Temple B in the Sacred
Precinct of Largo
Argentina.**

THE SACRED PRECINCT OF LARGO ARGENTINA

In this precinct stand four temples, of which only two were known from
ancient times. The others were discovered by chance during building work
in the 1920s. Fortunately their importance caused the authorities to sus-
pend work and the monuments were preserved. The most ancient of the
buildings is known as Temple C and dates from the late fourth or early third
century BC. It stands on a tall tuff plinth and is decorated with terracotta
ornaments. Its present appearance and the travertine paving of the whole
area are due to restoration under Domitian after a fire in 80 BC. The most
recent of the three other buildings, all from republican times, is Temple B.
It is circular and stands on a plinth with a flight of travertine steps in front.
Next to it have been found parts of a colossal acrolith of a female deity: the
head and neck alone are a metre and a half tall.

THE PANTHEON

The Pantheon was a temple originally built between 27 and 25 BC by Marcus Vipsanius Agrippa, Augustus's son-in-law, as part of his general improvements to the district. Its present appearance, however, is due to rebuilding under Hadrian.

The maker's stamp in the bricks enables the rebuilding to be dated to between 118 and 125 AD. The original building was radically modified, the orientation of the facade altered, and the great rotunda added. An inscription still legible on the architrave attributes the construction to Agrippa during his third consulship.

In late antiquity the Byzantine Emperor Phocas donated the monument to Pope Boniface IV, who in 609 turned it into the church of Santa Maria ad Matyres. As with other ancient buildings this conversion saved it from complete destruction, though alterations were made: the facade was raised on a flight of steps with a large rectangular porticoed square before it.

The great bronze portal, though much restored, may be the Roman original. The interior is dominated by the gigantic dome, 43.30 metres in diameter, the biggest masonry dome ever built.

The perfectly harmonious appearance of the building is due to its proportions: the distance between the floor and the summit of the dome is equal to its diameter, so creating a perfect sphere inside it.

The dome is decorated by five concentric tiers of coffering, which narrow to a circular opening almost 9 metres across. There are numerous recesses set in the walls which once contained the statues of gods and goddesses.

The Pantheon was dedicated to the twelve celestial deities and from them it took its name, since the Latin word *pantheon* derives from a Greek term composed of *pân* meaning "all" and *theòs* or "god."

Pantheon, views of the
exterior and the interior.

THE STADIUM OF DOMITIAN

Piazza Navona is one of the most important examples of continuity between ancient and modern Rome, and a fine example of urban design. Its elongated rectangular form, with one of the shorter sides curved, exactly repeats the design of the Stadium of Domitian.

This was constructed in about 86 AD for Greek athletic competitions. Measuring 275 metres long by over 10 in width, it had two tiers of seating which held up to three thousand spectators. The two principal entrance were in the middle of the longer sides and the race track itself was left completely clear.

Little remains of the rich sculptural decorations of the stadium, which must have included the statue of Pasquino, now on the corner of Palazzo Braschi in Piazza Pasquino. The obelisk incorporated by Gian Lorenzo Bernini in 1651 into the Fountain of the Rivers, at the centre of Piazza Navona, was brought from the Circus of Maxentius on the Via Appia, though probably it was originally part of a different monument.

View of Piazza Navona with Sant'Agnese in Agone, the Fountain of the Moor and the Fountain of the Four Rivers.

The stadium of Domitian on a coin minted by Septimius Severus in 202–203 AD to commemorate the return of the emperor and his son Caracalla as well as the latter's marriage to Plautilla. Games to celebrate the marriage were held in the stadium. British Museum, London.

THE TEMPLE OF HADRIAN

Construction of the Temple of Hadrian probably began in 139 AD, the year of the emperor's deification. Consecrated six years later, the building had eight columns on the shorter sides and fifteen on the longer.

The cell was decorated with a series of pillars with carvings representing the provinces of the empire: the surviving examples are now in the Musei Capitolini.

Eleven columns are still visible on the right side of the temple: their preservation is due to the reuse of the temple in the course of the centuries. Sixteenth-century drawings already show the columns incorporated into a sort of castle with numerous small windows.

The fundamental transformation dates from 1695, when the architect Francesco Fontana designed the Dogana di Terra (Customs House): he incorporated the surviving temple structures in the harmonious facade on his three-storey building, set with large windows. It is now the premises of the Rome Stock Exchange. Clearly visible inside are the remains of the *cella* (or main chamber) of the temple with its coffered barrel-vaulting.

Piazza Navona,
early twentieth century.

The Temple of Hadrian
in a photograph of 1868.

Coin of Innocent XII
with the Dogana di Terra.

THE COLUMN OF MARCUS AURELIUS

Erected between 180 (the date of the emperor's death) and 196 AD, this column records the feats of Marcus Aurelius against the Germans and Sarmatians.

An inscription states that in the latter year a certain Adrastus, the caretaker of the column, was authorised to reuse the wooden scaffolding to build himself a house.

The monument is modelled on Trajan's column. Nineteen circular blocks of stones set one above the other stand 100 Roman feet high (just under 30 metres). The tall base, decorated by a frieze with figures of Victory and a scene of submission by barbarians, was demolished in 1589 by Pope Sixtus V, who also replaced the emperor's statue at the top with the figure of St. Paul.

Two details of the carvings on the column of Marcus Aurelius.

Marcus Aurelius (161–180 AD). Musei Capitolini, Rome.

Antoninus Pius (138–161 AD). Museum of Sculpture, Munich.

The record of the deeds of Marcus Aurelius forms a continuous narrative spiralling round the shaft. The first carving shows the Roman army crossing the Danube by a bridge; this is followed by various dramatic episodes alternating with genre scenes. As on Trajan's column the figure of Victory divides the narrative into two parts, which probably depict the campaigns of 172–173 and 174–175 AD.

Apotheosis of Antoninus and Faustina, base of the Column of Antoninius Pius. Vatican Museums, Rome.

THE COLUMN OF ANTONINUS PIUS

When Antoninus Pius died, his adopted sons and successors Marcus Aurelius and Lucius Verus erected a monument to his honour in the Campus Martius, close by the place where the emperor's body was cremated. The marble base, decorated with carvings (now in the Vatican Museums), was surmounted by a red granite column designed by the architect Heracleides. The shaft of the column has been lost, except for the summit, which bore an inscription, the architect's signature and the date the stone was quarried. The rest was carved up and used to restore the nearby sundial of Augustus.

The principal relief on the base depicts the apotheosis of the emperor and his wife Faustina, borne to the sky by the winged genius Aion, the symbol of eternity. The two sides are decorated with almost identical scenes: a ring of cavalry encircling a parade of infantry, in allusion to the consecration of the imperial couple on the site of the funeral pyre.

THE ARA PACIS

The decision in 14 BC to build the Ara Pacis, the great altar of peace, and its consecration by Augustus five years later, is recounted by the emperor himself in his chronicle of his achievements.

During the reign of Hadrian, the marked rise in the height of the land around it made it necessary to isolate the monument with a retaining wall built out of bricks. From then on only the topmost strip remained visible with its figured frieze.

The monument, wholly of marble, was a rectangular enclosure with two great doors on the longer sides. It was set on a podium with access provided by a flight of steps. Inside this the altar proper stood on three steps running all the way round it; another five steps allowed the priest to reach the horizontal plane of the altar.

The rediscovery of the first fragments of the Ara Pacis date from 1568, when nine blocks of carved stone were found in the foundations of Palazzo Almagià. At various times in the nineteenth century further carvings were found and the monument was identified as the altar dedicated by Augustus.

In 1937-1938, to celebrate the second millennium of the emperor's birth, the Ara Pacis was reassembled and rebuilt not far from its original site. A new restoration and installation project, begun at the end of the last century, led in 2006 to the inauguration of a new setting designed by the American architect Richard Meier.

The Reliefs on the Ara Pacis

The Ara Pacis epitomised Augustus's policy and ideology, as well as the art of the age.

The processional frieze was the work of Greek artists inspired by the carvings on the Parthenon, the most celebrated monument of classical Greece.

Details of the reliefs on the Ara Pacis: Procession of the Quirites and (on the right) procession of the Julio-Claudian family.

Antonia Augusta as Venus Genetrix, commissioned by her son Claudius in 45 AD for the nymphaeum of the palace at Baia. Castello Aragonese, Baia Bacoli, Naples.

The Ara Pacis.

93. FROM THE CAMPUS MARTIUS TO THE MAUSOLEUM OF HADRIAN

The new building of the
Museum of the Ara Pacis
designed by Richard Meier.

94. FROM THE CAMPUS MARTIUS TO THE MAUSOLEUM OF HADRIAN

The lower part of the outside wall of the Ara Pacis is decorated with a frieze of vegetable motifs.

The upper part, flanking the entrance, has allegorical images that reflect the legend of the founding of Rome.

Reliefs at the sides depict the official procession held for consecration of the altar.

It opens with the lictors bearing the fasces, the emblem of authority, before the magistrate.

They are followed by the priests, including Augustus as Pontifex Maximus, and the imperial family, faithfully portrayed: we can identify Augustus's wife Livia with his sons Tiberius, the future emperor, and Drusus.

The procession depicted on the Ara Pacis was not so much the record of an actual event as the official representation of a dynasty.

The procession never took place as depicted, since in 14 BC, when it was decided to build the altar, Augustus was not yet Pontifex Maximus, and when the monument was consecrated in 9 BC his son-in-law Agrippa, depicted in the relief, had already died.

Detail of the carvings on the Ara Pacis: Mother Earth, the infant Gaius Caesar; Domitian and Domitia, the children of Antonia; Aeneas sacrificing to the Penates.

Bull-fight in the
Mausoleum of Augustus
in†a watercolour by
B. Pinelli (1781–1835).

Detail of the Mausoleum
of Augustus in a drawing
by G.B. Piranesi
(1720–1778).

96. FROM THE CAMPUS MARTIUS TO THE MAUSOLEUM OF HADRIAN

THE MAUSOLEUM OF AUGUSTUS

The Mausoleum
of Augustus today.

In 29 BC, after conquering Egypt and visiting Alexander the Great's tomb in Alexandria, Augustus began construction of his own mausoleum as a great dynastic sepulchre for himself and his descendants. The edifice is circular and measures about 87 metres across. The door is flanked by two pillars, to which were fixed the bronze tables with Augustus's autobiography, and two obelisks, perhaps commissioned by the emperor himself: one now stands between the statues of the Dioscuri before the Quirinal, the other by the apse of Santa Maria Maggiore.

Throughout the first century AD the mausoleum was used as a tomb for the imperial family.

In the Middle Ages it was converted to various uses and in quite modern times it was used for public entertainments. Excavations in the 1930s cleared away all the later additions to reveal the original structure.

FORUM BOARIUM AND FORUM HOLITORIUM IN HISTORY

The plain between the Tiber and the Palatine, Aventine and Capitoline hills was very important early in the city's history and perhaps in even more primitive times.

On this strip of territory there intersected two of the principal lines of communication of central Italy: the Tiber, navigable as far as Orte, and a road linking Campania with Etruria, crossing the Tiber at the Insula Tiberina by the Sublician bridge, the first to span the river. The same area was also traversed by the Via Salaria, used by the pastoral population of the Sabine hills to bring salt from the river mouth.

In archaic times the plain grew into an important trading centre, above all for goods arriving by water, with thriving cattle and vegetable markets, the Forum Boarium and Forum Holitorium.

The first conspicuous buildings were erected by a king of Etruscan origins, Servius Tullius (sixth century BC), but the most important phase of construction came in the second century BC after the area was ravaged by fire. It was then that the first warehouse was built (the *Horrea Aemiliana*), probably by Scipio Aemilianus, replaced in the imperial period by a complex of brick buildings.

The Arch of the Argentarii, perhaps originally an entrance to the Forum Boarium, stands near the church of San Giorgio al Velabro. The monument was dedicated by the bankers and cattle dealers to Septimius Severus and his family in 204 AD.

The Arch of the Argentarii, like that of Septimius Severus, bears traces of the obliterated figures of Geta and, probably, Caracalla's wife Plautilla and her father, all assassinated by the emperor. Before the church of San Giorgio stands a great four-sided arch erected by Constans II in 357 AD when he visited Rome.

The arch is cross-vaulted and the keystones of the four arches are decorated with the figures of goddesses: Roma and Juno (both seated), Minerva and perhaps Ceres (standing).

The attic, well preserved till 1830, was demolished in the belief it was mediaeval work.

THE SACRED PRECINCT OF SAINT OMOBONO

At the foot of the Capitol lies a sacred precinct that includes two small temples dedicated to Fortune and the Mater Matuta, traditionally attributed to the period of Servius Tullius. Archaeological studies have confirmed the accounts of ancient writers by revealing a more ancient level dating from the later seventh or early sixth century BC, in which the only sign of cult use is an altar.

The presence of an Etruscan inscription and a small ivory votive offering bearing the name of a member of the Spurinna family, originally of Tarquinia, is important evidence of the Etruscan presence in Rome.

It probably confirms indirectly the tradition of the dynasty of the Tarquins. The two temples, founded in about the mid-sixth century BC, were reconstructed a number of times in the republican period, always by person-

ages in some way connected with the Etruscan world, such as Camillus
after his conquest of Veii in 396 BC.

TEMPLES OF THE FORUM HOLITORIUM

The small square now bounded by the Tiber, the Theatre of Marcellus and
the Capitol was once the ancient Forum Holitorium, the vegetable market
where, in republican times, four temples stood, dedicated to Janus, Spes
(Hope), Juno Sospita and Pietas (this last was demolished to build the
Theatre of Marcellus).
The imposing remains of the first three edifices stand beside the church
of San Nicola in Carcere, partly built over them. The podium and colonnade
of the Temple of Juno Sospita can be seen in the undercroft and in the front
of the church.
The northernmost temple, dedicated to Janus, is the best preserved, complete with a frieze. It is incorporated in the right side of the church of San
Nicola.

TEMPLES OF THE FORUM BOARIUM

The Forum Boarium, covering most of the plain between the Tiber and the
Capitol, Palatine and Aventine, contains two exceptionally well-preserved
little temples in what is now Piazza Bocca della Verità. The Temple of Fortune, actually identified as the temple of Portunus (an ancient tutelary God
of Rome's first trading port, the Portus Tiberinus, on the bend in the river),
was erected in the early monarchical period and rebuilt a number of times
by the first century AD.
The temple stands on a drystone plinth. The elevation is entirely made out
of Anio tuff (volcanic stone), except for the columns and capitals which are
of travertine.
The cornice is original and bears lion protomes. The circular Temple of
Vesta nearby is wholly built out of Greek marble from Mount Pentelicus.
Erected by a wealthy Roman oil merchant, it was in fact dedicated to Hercules, the patron of oil-sellers. Ancient records refer to it as the Temple of
Hercules Victor.
It stands on a stepped stone base, with a ring of twenty Corinthian columns
encircling a cell with the entrance on the east side. It seems to have been
the work of Hermodoros, a Greek architect from Salamis active in Rome in
the later second century BC.

Architectural detail of the Temple of Juno Sospita.

The church of San Nicola in Carcere superimposed on the Temple of Juno Sospita.

The Temple of Portunus, Forum Boarium.

The Temple of Vesta, Forum Boarium.

Castel Sant'Angelo and Ponte Sant'Angelo.

Detail of the base of the castle in which appears the masonry of the Mausoleum of Hadrian.

Hadrian (117–138 AD). Israel Museum, Jerusalem.

Ponte Sant'Angelo, perspective view with Castel Sant'Angelo.

THE MAUSOLEUM OF HADRIAN

The monumental tomb built by the Emperor Hadrian on the right bank of the Tiber was inspired by the Mausoleum of Augustus in the Campus Martius.

To connect the mausoleum with the city Hadrian erected in Aemilian Bridge, now much altered but still in use and called Ponte Sant'Angelo.

The mausoleum consisted originally of a base in the form of a parallelepiped, 84 metres wide and 10 high, on which rested a circular drum 64 metres across and 20 high.

The whole structure was sheathed in marble and travertine and covered with a mound of earth planted with trees and ringed with statues. On the summit stood a four-horse chariot with the statue of Hadrian. For almost a century, down to the time of Caracalla, the mausoleum was the burial place of the emperors.

Transformed into a fortress in the Middle Ages it became the strong point of the Vatican's defensive system and was also used as a prison. In the Renaissance the mausoleum took the name by which it is now known, Castel Sant'Angelo, when the statue of an angel replaced Hadrian's on the summit of the monument.

PUBLIC WORKS

On the previous pages
Mosaic pavement,
Baths of Caracalla.

The Via Appia Antica.

Baths of Diocletian,
exterior view of the aulae
between the frigidarium
and the southeast gymnasium.

THE BATHS IN HISTORY

Everyone – men and women, young and old, rich and poor – went to the baths or *thermae*. The wealthy, though they had private baths of their own, were actually assiduous visitors to the public baths, where they went accompanied by their slaves and "clients" (free men who offered their services in exchange for patronage). The clients would attend their patron at the baths, helping to perfume him with oil and invigorate him with massages.

Even the emperor and members of his family went to public baths and mingled with the crowds. Admission was cheap, in some cases free of charge. The aediles were responsible for ensuring they functioned properly, controlling hygiene, the temperatures inside and the contracts with suppliers.

Under the republic it was not thought necessary to bathe more than once a week but under the empire many people bathed daily. Habits, of course, varied. We know that Augustus did not care to bathe often in winter but Commodus had seven or eight baths every day; and Gordian took four or five baths daily in summer and two in winter.

At the baths it was possible to follow different routines. Bathers would normally strip in the changing room and

The Baths of Diocletian, gymnasium.

The Baths of Diocletian, gymnasium.

Conjectural reconstruction of the interior of the Baths of Diocletian in a watercolour by E. Paulin (1848–1915). Ecole des Beaux-Arts, Paris.

proceed to the gymnasium, where they oiled their bodies and performed exercises. From there they passed to the sweat bath (*laconicum*), and so to a hot pool (*calidarium*) and a room with small tubs filled with lukewarm water (*tepidarium*). The last stages were a large unheated chamber, often richly decorated (*frigidarium*), and the outdoor swimming pool (*natatio*).

THE BATHS OF DIOCLETIAN

The baths of Diocletian, the biggest ever built in Rome, were erected in one of the most densely populated parts of the city, the area comprising the Esquiline, Quirinal and Viminal hills. Many buildings were demolished to make way for this immense complex, built rapidly between 298 and 306 AD and covering 140,000 square metres. The central building measured 250 by 180 metres.

Some parts of the baths can still be seen, incorporated into more recent buildings. For example the church of Santa Maria degli Angeli was built in the central chamber of the baths and its entrance in set in one of the apses of the *calidarium*. The areas of the basilica which were originally part

of the baths have been incorporated into the museum of the baths (Museo delle Terme). Its garden still contains the facade of the main building.

The Baths of Diocletian.

THE BATHS OF TITUS

The only comprehensive record we have of the baths which the Emperor Titus inaugurated in 80 AD is a plan drawn by the sixteenth-century architect Andrea Palladio.

The complex was not very large and had the same orientation as Nero's Domus Aurea, which adjoined it on the east. Access was provided by a flight of steps on the side facing the Colosseum.

The extreme rapidity of its construction, mentioned by the poet Martial, and its close connection with Nero's palace next door, suggest that it was simply a conversion of the sumptuous baths of the Domus Aurea. This would reflect the policy of Vespasian and his sons, who sought to restore to public use the extravagant and luxurious buildings erected by Nero for himself. Its plan is typical of all large public baths, with a central basilica and two identical suites of chambers ranged on each side of it.

THE BATH OF TRAJAN

The baths of Trajan were designed, like the emperor's other public works, by the architect Apollodorus of Damascus. He erected the new complex over the remains of the Domus Aurea, destroyed by fire in 104 AD. The baths were opened five years later.

They covered an area of over 100,000 square metres, almost half of which was occupied by the central building. Trajan's were the first large baths where the principal building was flanked by an outer court with an exedra, a model imitated in all subsequent large bathing complexes. Some remains of Trajan's Baths can be found in the park on the Oppian hill.

THE BATHS OF CARACALLA

The Thermae Antoninianae, the best preserved baths of the imperial period, were built by Caracalla, who dedicated the central building in 216 AD. The outer enclosure was completed by the last emperors of the house of Severus, Heliogabalus and Alexander Severus.

Water was piped from a special offshoot of the Aqua Marcia known as the Aqua Antoniniana, brought to the baths across the Appian Way not far from Porta San Sebastiana.

The Baths of Caracalla could accommodate up to 1600 bathers, about half the number of the later Baths of Diocletian. Renewed by the Emperors Aurelian and Diocletian and by Theodoric, king of the Visigoths, it ceased to function in 537, when the Goths blocked the aqueducts and cut off the water supply.

Excavations through the centuries, above all the sixteenth, revealed the rich decoration and furnishings of the complex, like the two granite baths now in Piazza Farnese.

View of the Baths of Caracalla, frigidarium, eastern gymnasium, calidarium and adjacent halls.

The Baths of Caracalla, detail of mosaic decoration.

THE PORT ON THE TIBER

The most ancient port of Rome was on the right bank of the Tiber, in the bend facing the Velabrum district and the Forum Boarium. This was a cramped area which allowed no scope for expansion. After the third Punic war (late third century BC) the city's population grew rapidly, trade flourished, and it became urgent to find a site for a new port. The choice fell on the great open plain which stretched before the Aventine, and here new docks and warehouses were erected.

Behind the port, towards the Aurelian Walls, stood the *Mons Testaceus* (meaning "Hill of Potsherds"). This was a completely artificial hill, 50 metres high and about 1 kilometre around the base. It already existed in Augustan times, but most of the material dates from between 140 BC and the third century AD, being built up by the gradual accumulation of fragments of jars containing products that arrived by water at the port of Rome. Carts would climb a ramp to the hilltop to dispose of their "empties", jars valueless once their contents had been removed. This small hill consists almost exclusively of fragments of oil jars from Betica,

The Insula Tiberina
with the river in full spate
in 1986.

Tiberina Island
with the Fabrician
and Cestian bridges.

Apollo of the Tiber, copy from
the age of Hadrian or the
Antonines of a classical
Greek original. The statue
was found in the bed of the
river when the embankments
were being rebuilt. Palazzo
Massimo alle Terme, Museo
Nazionale Romano, Rome.

115. PUBLIC WORKS

now Andalusia, and the coasts of Mediterranean Africa. Often they bear their maker's mark, and painted on the side of the jars is the name of the exporter and the seals applied on departure and arrival.

THE ISLAND IN THE TIBER

When the plague was raging at Rome in 293 BC, the *Sibylline Books* were consulted and an embassy was sent to Epidaurus in Greece, the centre of the cult of Aesculapius, the god of medicine. Two years later a Roman trireme returned to the homeland bringing one of the sacred serpents, the symbol of the god. The snake escaped and swam from the military port on the banks of the Campus Martius to the Insula Tiberina, the island in the Tiber, where it disappeared. This was taken as an omen that a new temple to Aesculapius should be built on the island and construction began in 289 BC.
The use of the Insula Tiberina as a sanatorium, probably due to its isolation from the city, continued throughout the Middle Ages and it is still the location of the Fatebenefratelli Hospital, founded in 1548.
The islet was the object of general redevelopment in the middle of the first century BC. Bridges linking it to the mainland were built and the eastern tip was refashioned in the form of a ship's prow, so that the island itself was transformed into the image of the trireme that brought the sacred serpent, which is also represented entwined around a rod in the hand of Aesculapius.

THE BRIDGES

The most ancient bridge built over the Tiber was the wooden Sublician Bridge, close to the Forum Boarium, which linked the far side of the Tiber and the Janiculum with the rest of the city. Tradition has it that the Sublician was the bridge that Horatius Cocles held agains an Etruscan army under Porsenna, so allowing the Romans time to hew down its timbers and prevent the enemy entering the city.
The most ancient stone bridge was the Aemilian, built in 179 BC. Some arches of this bridge are still visible just below the Insula Tiberina. This was

Boat on a sea swarming with fish: fragment of a fresco from excavations at the river port of San Paolo a Lungotevere Pietra Papa. The painting dates from 125–150 AD.

The Ponte Rotto and the Insula Tiberina.

The Cestian Bridge and the Insula Tiberina.

followed by the Milvian (or Mulvian) bridge built by Marcus Aemilius Scaurus in 109 BC, probably to replace the wooden bridge built some hundred years earlier to bring the Via Flaminia across the Tiber north of Rome. It was here that Constantine in 312 BC won his final victory over his rival Maxentius.

THE CITY WALLS

According to tradition, the city's first walls were built by the sixth king of Rome, Servius Tullius (sixth century BC), but the powerful circle of what is now called the "Servian Wall" was erected following the Gallic invasion. The walls were built out of tuff from quarries acquired by Rome after the conquest of Veii (396 BC).
They enclosed an area of 426 hectares and were rebuilt on a number of occasions between the fourth century BC and 87 BC (during the civil war

From left to right
The Ponte Sistino.

The Fabrician Bridge.

View of the Tiber with the Sistine bridge and the dome of St. Peter's in the background.

The Milvian Bridge.

between Marius and Sulla). They were frequently repaired, before falling gradually into disuse and then being deliberately levelled in the Augustan period.

The city remained practically without walls until 271 AD, when the Emperor Aurelian decided it was advisable to fortify Rome against barbarian incursions, above all in the long periods when wars kept him abroad. The work went ahead rapidly and by the time of Aurelian's death in 275 most of the wall must have been built. It fell to his successor Probus to complete the work.

This wall, made of brick, was 6 metres high and 3.50 metres thick. It was fortified with square towers every hundred *passi* (equal to 29.60 metres). Its length was just under 19 kilometres and it took in numerous earlier edifices. The first emperor to strengthen it was Maxentius, but the most massive enlargement was the work of Arcadius and Honorius. Facing attacks by the Goths in 401–402 they doubled the wall's height; the path along

The Ponte Rotto.

On the following pages
Sunset over Aqua Claudia
Roman Aqueduct,
Parco degli Acquedotti.

its top patrolled by guards was replaced by a covered gallery and the Mausoleum of Hadrian was included in the fortification as a castle outpost on the right bank of the Tiber.

One of the most ancient structures incorporated into Aurelian's Walls was the pyramid of Caius Cestius, erected under the provisions of his testament in less than 330 days. The bronze statues of Caius Cestius, now in the Musei Capitolini, were paid for with money from the sale of tapestries from Pergamum, which could not be placed in the sepulchre because of a sumptuary law of 18 BC.

THE GATES

In Aurelian's project the main gates set in the walls consisted of twin entrances, covered with arches and contained within two semi-circular towers. More modest entrances were simply inserted in the stretches of walls between two square towers.

The Aurelian Walls and the Pyramid of Caius Cestius.

Aurelian Walls, Porta Maggiore and the tomb of Eurysaces (circa 30 BC).

Detail of the Aurelian Walls.

Porta Maggiore seen from the outside.

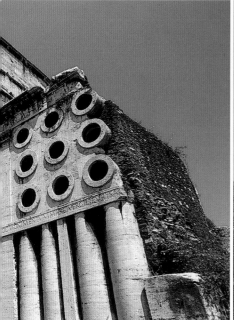

In the course of the reinforcements decided by Arcadius and Honorius many of the double entrances were eliminated and the towers were raised and fortified. The gates, with an inner counter-door; were transformed into self-sufficient fortresses. The closure was doubled and consisted on the outside of a double gate and on the inside of a portcullis which could be raised and lowered.

One of the best preserved stretches of the Aurelian Walls between Porta Latina and Porta San Sebastiano, with the Museo delle Mura (Museum of the City Walls). Here it is also possible to walk along the top of a section of the walls.

THE AQUEDUCTS

The water supply in the great cities of the empire and Rome above all was so advanced that only modern industrialised nations have ever surpassed Roman achievements. Rome's first aqueduct was built in the fourth cen-

Porta San Giovanni, set in the Aurelian walls in 1574.

Porta San Paolo.

tury BC to bring water from Paeneste; in the imperial period a million cubic metres of water flowed daily into the city down eleven aqueducts, a quantity only surpassed by modern Rome in the 1970s.

The most celebrated Roman aqueduct was the one begun by Caligula and later completed by Claudius. The canal started from Subiaco and reached Rome after travelling over 68 kilometres. For a stretch of about 16 kilometres it was carried on magnificent tuff arches still visible in the countryside near the city gates.

An offshoot leading to the Caelius was begun by Nero, while Domitian continued it as far as the Palatine.

THE CONSULAR ROADS

The first true paved road outside Rome was the Appian Way, constructed in 312 BC by the Censor Appius Claudius Caecus to join Rome to Capua and later Brindisi. The technique for building these and other Roman roads was extremely precise and, as can still be seen, they were made to last. The first step in construction was to dig two shallow parallel trenches marking the sides of the road, which had to be at least wide enough for two carts to pass by each other. Then the roadway was dug out and foundations laid of sand and lime. This was covered for up to 1.5 metres with layers of four different materials: a bed of large stones (*statumen*), smaller stones and lime (*rudus*), sand and gravel (*nucleus*), and then a carefully laid surface of smoothed paving stones (*summum dorsum*). The roads were slightly cambered to improve runoff.

Between the third and second centuries BC other important roads were built to connect Rome with her newly conquered territories; they included the Via Cassia, Via Aurelia and Via Flaminia. The growth of the road network kept pace with the expansion of empire and the maintenance of the roads was a constant concern of all emperors.

Porta Pinciana: seen from the inside.

The Claudian Aqueduct.

Pyramid of Caius Cestius incorporated into the Aurelian Walls.

Casal Rotondo, sepulchre of the Augustan period.

The Villa of the Quintilii.

THE
MUSEUMS

On the previous pages
Fragments of the colossal
Statue of Constantine.
Courtyard, Palazzo
dei Conservatori, Rome.

*Equestrian Statue of Marcus
Aurelius.* Esedra di Marco
Aurelio, Palazzo
dei Conservatori, Rome.

Palazzo Nuovo, Sala degli
Imperatori.

The *Capitoline She-Wolf.*
Etruscan bronze, early fifth
century BC. The twins,
Romulus and Remus, were
probably added in the
fifteenth century. Musei
Capitolini, Rome.

ROME AND ITS MUSEUMS

It was in the Renaissance that museums were first created to display the immense wealth of Roman remains. They were exhibited in the palaces which still house the Vatican Museums and the Musei Capitolini.
In 1899 the new Italian State instituted the Museo Nazionale Romano to house the immense number of relics and works of art being turned up in the new excavations. The Museo Nazionale Romano has recently been reorganised and is now divided between four different buildings. The collections at Palazzo Altemps are dedicated to antiquarian collecting. Palazzo Massimo alle Terme has displays of frescoes, sculptures, mosaics and other items from late republican to late imperial times, as well as a large section of coins and jewellery. In the Baths of Diocletian some of the ancient interiors, still in fair condition, and the buildings that surround the cloisters of Michelangelo contain exhibits ordered by the following themes: the city's foundation and early development; figurative art in the republican period; art and social classes; the history of the Latin language and writing. The Museo della Crypta Balbi is organised as two sections illustrating the history of the site from antiquity to the twentieth century and the transformations of the city of Rome between the fifth and ninth centuries.

Man in a Toga, the proud symbol of Roman citizenship imposed by Augustus, with images of his ancestors (50–40 BC). Centrale Montemartini, Musei Capitolini, Rome Rome.

The *Esquiline Venus*, a sculpture associated with the cult of Isis, from the first century BC. Centrale Montemartini, Musei Capitolini, Rome Rome.

Boy Removing a Thorn from His Foot, bronze from the first century BC. Sala dei Trionfi, Appartamento dei Conservatori, Musei Capitolini, Rome.

The central archaeological precinct has the Museo Palatino and the Antiquarium Forense, which houses archaeological remains found in the Roman Forum, including the famous frieze from the Basilica Aemilia.

A small collection of ancient sculptures, mostly from the Roman period, is in the Museo Baracco on Corso Vittorio Emanuele II.

A very different kind of collection, above all interesting for educational purposes, is in the Museo della Civiltà Romana, housed in an imposing edifice in the EUR district. Its exhibits are almost exclusively reproductions which illustrate the history of the ancient nucleus of the city and various aspects of Roman civilisation. The exhibits are arranged chronologically. Of special interest is the model designed by the architects Italo Gismondi for the Mostra Augustea della Romanità (1937). The model covers about 200 square metres (on a scale of 1:250) and reproduces the city in the age of Constantine. The museum is currently closed.

THE MUSEI CAPITOLINI

This is the world's oldest public museum. Founded in 1471 by Pope Sixtus IV, it was opened to the public by Clement XII in the early eighteenth century. The collections of the Musei Capitolini, now owned by the City of Rome, include some outstandingly famous and important pieces, like the *Capito-*

Capitoline Brutus. Sala dei Trionfi, Appartamento dei Conservatori, Musei Capitolini, Rome.

line *She-Wolf*, the *Capitoline Venus* and the group of *Cupid and Psyche*. Some of the sculptures and other exhibits were installed in the late nineties in the Centrale Montemartini, the city's first thermo-electric power station, on the Via Ostiense. The installation of the ancient relics alongside early twentieth-century industrial machinery made such a powerful impact that the exhibition has been turned into a permanent display.

A particularly important exhibit in the Capitoline collections is the equestrian statue of Marcus Aurelius. This is one of the few bronze statues that has survived intact from ancient times. The decision not to melt it down for the sake of the bronze was probably due to the mistaken identification of the figure as Constantine, an emperor greatly revered in the Middle Ages because he was believed to have embraced Christianity. The figure of Marcus Aurelius on horseback almost certainly commemorates the triumph he was awarded for his victory over the Parthians, celebrated in Rome in 166 AD.

The statue was long kept in the Basilica of San Giovanni in Laterano before being chosen by Michelangelo as the centrepiece of Piazza del Campidoglio (on the Capitol). Removed from its original position in order to preserve it better, the original statue of Marcus Aurelius is now visible in the great new glazed gallery constructed in the "Roman Garden" of Palazzo dei Conservatori, while a copy has been installed in the centre of the piazza.

THE VATICAN MUSEUMS

The Vatican Museums and the Papal Galleries (Gallerie Pontifiche del Vaticano) form an outstandingly important museum complex by both the richness of their exhibits and the splendid setting.

The holdings in the Museo Pio-Clementino, Museo Chiaramonti, Braccio Nuovo, Museo Egizio, and Museo Etrusco together form the world's largest collection of ancient art.

The beginnings go back to the Renaissance popes, who displayed the core of the collection in the Belvedere Courtyard.

The original collection was depleted by gifts from the popes to the city of Rome and foreign sovereigns.

The museum was reorganised by the popes of the eighteenth and nineteenth centuries.

The Vatican Museums contain many outstandingly important and famous works, including the *Laocoön*, the base of the Column of Antoninus Pius, the two porphyry sarcophagi of St. Helena and Constantia, respectively mother and daughter of the Emperor Constantine, the *Apollo Belvedere*, the statue of Augustus from Prima Porta, and many others. There are also extensive Etruscan remains, including the furnishings of the Regolini-Galassi tomb and the bronze statue of the Mars of Todi.

THE MUSEO NAZIONALE ROMANO
Palazzo Massimo alle terme

The collection at Palazzo Massimo alle Terme forms part of the Museo Nazionale Romano.

It mainly displays material from the splendid houses of the senatorial class in Rome.

Tiberius as Emperor.
Vatican Museums, Rome.

The *Apoxyomenos*, Roman copy (first century AD) of a Greek original by the sculptor Lysippus (circa 320 BC). Vatican Museums, Rome.

The *Apollo Belvedere*, copy of a Greek original of the fourth century BC. Vatican Museums, Rome.

The *Laocoön*, exhibited in a niche of the Belvedere Courtyard. Vatican Museums, Rome.

Viridarium, 30–20 BC, Livia's Villa at Prima Porta (Rome). Palazzo Massimo alle Terme, Museo Nazionale Romano, Rome.

These works, when viewed together with the items from the imperial palaces displayed at the Museo Palatino, provide a comprehensive panorama of the art of late republican and imperial Rome.

The second floor of the palace is wholly devoted to a display of the most significant examples of Roman decorative painting and mosaic pavements found in Rome and Lazio.

The display includes reconstructions of some interiors of important residential complexes, such as Livia's villa at Prima Porta and the Villa della Farnesina on Via della Lungara.

In particular the reconstruction of some interiors, with the frescoes on the walls and stuccoed vaulting, reveals the conceptual unity of the decoration, which is usually seen only as fragments.

The ground floor of Palazzo Massimo contains examples of iconography and portraiture from the late republican period, with a display of sculptural decorations from the residences of the wealthy classes. Many statues are Roman copies of Greek originals by great sculptors such as Lysippus and Praxiteles (both fourth century BC).

The basement level has sections devoted to numismatics, covering ancient times, the Middle Ages and the present, and a display of jewels and household items made of precious materials, mostly from imperial times. The artefacts mainly come from tombs regularly excavated, so they can be analysed in their cultural and historical setting and not viewed merely as collectors' pieces. Among the exhibits is an unusual example of the em-

Lysippus school, *Pugilist*, circa 330 BC. Palazzo Massimo alle Terme, Museo Nazionale Romano, Rome.

The Galatian Suicide from the Ludovisi collection. It has recently been suggested that this statue and *The Dying Gaul* (now in the Musei Capitolini) both stood in the octagonal chamber of the Domus Aurea. Palazzo Altemps, Museo Nazionale Romano, Rome.

The *Ludovisi Throne*, depicting the birth of Aphrodite Urania, from the fifth century BC. Palazzo Altemps, Museo Nazionale Romano, Rome.

One of the daughters of Niobe (440–430 BC). Palazzo Massimo alle Terme, Museo Nazionale Romano, Rome.

balmed body of a little girl with her tomb furnishings from Grottarossa (second century BC).

Palazzo Altemps

In the second half of the sixteenth century Cardinal Altemps decided to transform the family palace, under construction for a century, into "a home for statues."

Subsequently, however, the cardinal's collection of ancient sculptures and his rich library were dispersed, a destiny shared by the majority of the patrician collections, which frequently changed hands.

With the restructuring of the building in the late 1990s, it proved possible to recreate the original Cinquecento interior.

It now contains sixteen sculptures that once belonged to the Altemps collection and items from other important collections, like the Boncompagni Ludovisi and Mattei collections and the Egyptian collection of the Museo Nazionale Romano. The antiquarian reconstruction of the original Cinquecento setting was suggested by the close relations between the Ludovisi collection and the sculptures owned by the Altemps family, due to changes of ownership of some pieces.

Restoration of the interiors also enables visitors to admire not only the splendid statues but also, in their museum walkthrough, the magnificent building that houses them.

APPENDIX

WHERE TO EAT
AND WHERE TO STAY

As a guide to your stay in Rome, to choose itineraries or where to eat and sleep, scan this code with your smartphone.

On the previous pages
Church of Santa Costanza, mosaics
in the circular vault, early 4th century.

WHERE TO EAT

Price range

For a three-course meal for one with half a bottle of wine (or equivalent meal) taxes and extra charges.
– €   under 30 €
– €€   30 €-40 €
– €€€   40 €-50 €
– €€€€   50 €-60 €
– €€€€€   over 60 €
Unless otherwise stated, all restaurant accept credit cards and serve vegetarian meals.

Piazza Navona

Da Francesco
Piazza del Fico 29
06 6864 009
Disabled access
€

Terra di Siena
Piazza Pasquino 77-78
06 6830 7704
Closed Sun
€€

Lilli
Via Tor di Nona 26
06 686 1916
Closed Mon, Sun dinner
€

Convivio Troiani
Vicolo dei Soldati 31
06 686 9432
Closed Sun, Mon lunch
€€€€€

Cul de Sac
Piazza Pasquino 73
€€€€

Pizzeria La Montecarlo
Vicolo Savelli 12
06 686 1877
€

Tre Archi
Via dei Coronari 233
06 686 5890
Closed Sun
€

Fraterna Domus
Via di Monte Brianzo 62
06 6880 5475
Closed Thu
€

Zio Ciro
Via della Pace 1
06 686 4802
€

Antica Taverna
Via Monte Giordano 12
06 6880 1053
€

Pantheon

L'Eau Vive
Via Monterone 85
06 6880 1095
Closed Sun
€€

Il Bacaro
Via degli Spagnoli 27
06 687 2554
€€

Osteria dell'Ingegno
Piazza di Pietra 45
06 678 0662
€€

Enoteca Corsi
Via del Gesù 87
06 679 0821
Closed Sun
€

Maccheroni
Piazza delle Coppelle 44
06 6830 7895
€€

Ristorante Boccondivino
Piazza in Campo Marzio 6
06 6830 8626
Closed Sun
€€€

Trattoria
Via del Pozzo delle Cornacchie 25
333 468 9106
Closed Sun
€€€

Settimio all'Arancio
Via dell'Arancio 50-52
06 687 6119
Closed Sun
€

Da Gino
Vicolo Rosini 4
06 687 3434
Closed Sun
€

Obikà
Piazza di Firenze 26A
06 683 2630
€

Campo de' Fiori to the Capitol

Piperno
Via Monte de' Cenci 9
06 6880 6629
Closed Sun dinner, Mon
€€€

Da Giggetto
Via del Portico d'Ottavia
06 686 1105
Closed Mon
€€€

Vecchia Roma
Piazza Campitelli 18
06 686 4604
Closed Wed, two weeks Aug
€€€€

La Taverna del Ghetto
Via Portico d'Ottavia 8
06 6880 9771
Closed Fri dinner, Sat lunch
€€

Sora Margherita
Piazza delle Cinque Scole 30
06 687 4216
Closed Sun dinner, Tue
No credit cards
€€

Ba' Ghetto
Via del Portico d'Ottavia 57
06 6889 2868
Closed Fri dinner, Sat lunch
€€

Filetti di Baccalà
Largo dei Librari 88
06 686 4018
Closed Sun
No credit cards
€

Da Sergio alle Grotte
Vicolo delle Grotte 27
06 686 4293
Closed Sun
€€

Osteria ar Galletto
Piazza Farnese 104
06 686 1714
Closed Sun
€

Yotvata
Piazza Cenci 70
06 6813 4481
Closed Fri dinner, Sat lunch
€€

The Spanish Steps & Villa Borghese

Fiaschetteria Beltramme
(da Cesaretto)
Via della Croce 39
Closed Sun
No credit cards
€

Edy
Vicolo del Babuino 4
06 600 1738
Closed Sun, Mon lunch
€€

Gusto
Piazza Augusto Imperatore 9
06 322 6273
€€€

Antica Birreria Peroni
Via San Marcello 19/piazza
Ss. Apostoli
06 679 5310
Closed Sun
€

Oliver Glowig
Palazzo Aldrovandi,
Via Aldrovandi 15
06 321 6126
Closed Sun, Mon
€€€€€

Osteria Margutta
Via Margutta 82
06 323 1025
Closed Sun, Mon lunch
€€

Hosteria St Ana
Via della Penna 68-69
06 361 0291
Closed Sun, Mon lunch
€€

Al 34
Via Mario de' Fiori 34
06 679 5091
Closed Mon
€€

Il Brillo Parlante
Via della Fontanella 12
06 324 3334
€

Mare
Via di Ripetta 242
06 890 17481
€€€

Ancient Rome

Checchino dal 1887
Via di Monte Testaccio 30
06 574 6318
Closed Sun, Mon
€€€€

Agustarello
Via G. Branca 100
06 574 6585
Closed Sun
No credit cards
€

Da Remo
Piazza S. Maria Liberatrice 44
06 574 6270
Closed Sun
€

Volpetti
Via Marmorata 47
06 574 4306
Closed Sun
€

Felice
Via Mastro Giorgio 29
06 574 6800
€€€

Osteria Degli Amici
Via Zabaglia 25
06 578 1466
Closed Tue
Disabled access
€€

Da Bucatino
Via della Robbia 84-86
06 574 6886
Closed Mon
Disabled access
€€

Acqua e Farina
Piazza O. Giustiniani 2
06 574 1382
€

Il Seme e la Foglia
Via Galvani 18
06 574 3008
No credit cards
€

Né Arte né Parte
Via della Robbia 15-17
06 575 0279
Closed Mon
€€

The Esquiline & Lateran

Agata e Romeo
Via Carlo Alberto 45
06 446 6115
Closed Sat lunch, Sun, Mon lunch
Disabled access
€€€€€

Pompi
Via Albalonga 7B/9/11
06 700 0418
€

Cannavota
Piazza S. Giovanni in Laterano 20
06 7720 5007
Closed Aug
Disabled access
€€

Trattoria Monti
Via di San Vito 13A
06 446 6573
Closed Mon, Sun dinner, Aug
€€

F.I.S.H.
Via dei Serpenti 16
06 4782 4962
Closed lunch, Mon, Aug
€€€

Al Maharajah
Via dei Serpenti 124
06 474 7144
Disabled access
€€

Hang Zhou
Via Principe Eugenio 82
06 487 2732
Disabled access
€

Enoteca Cavour 313
Via Cavour 313
06 678 5496
Closed Sun in summer
€

L'Angolo di Napoli
Via Agostino Depretis 77A
06 474 6866
Closed Sun lunch, Mon
€€

Il Guru
Via Cimarra 4-6
06 474 4110
Closed lunch
€€

The Quirinal & Via Veneto

Caffè Veneto
Via Veneto 120
06 482 7107
Closed Mon
Disabled access
€€€€€

La Scala
Via di S. Isidoro 5
06 481 9264
Closed Tue
€€€

La Giara
Via Toscana 46, at Via Sardegna
06 4274 5421
Closed Sun lunch in summer,
also Sun dinner in winter, Aug
Disabled access
€€€

Colline Emiliane
Via degli Avignonesi 22
06 481 7538
Closed Sun dinner, Mon
Disabled access
€€

Andrea
Via Sardegna 28
06 4821 819/4740 557
Closed Sat lunch, Sun
Disabled access
€€€€

Trimani
Via Cernaia 37/B
06 446 9630
Closed Sun
Disabled access
€€

La Gallina Bianca
Via A. Rosmini 9
06 474 3777
Disabled access
€

Dagnino
Via Vittorio Emanuele Orlando 75
and Via Torino 95
06 481 8660
Disabled access
€

Sapori Sardi
Via Piemonte 79
06 474 5256
Disabled access
€€

Africa
Via Gaeta 26
06 494 1077
Closed Mon
Disabled access
€

Trastevere & Prati

Cheap Eats

Da Augusto
Piazza de' Renzi 15
06 580 3798
Closed Sat dinner, Sun
No credit cards
€

Il Rugantino
Via della Lungaretta 54
06 581 8517
€€

La Tana de Noantri
Via della Paglia 1-3, off Piazza
Santa Maria in Trastevere
06 580 6404
Closed Tue
€

Pizzeria da Ivo
Via S. Francesco a Ripa 158
06 581 7082
Closed lunch, Tue
€

Sorpasso
Via Properzio 31–33
06 890 24554
Closed Sun
€

Pizzeria dar Poeta
Vicolo del Bologna 45-46
06 588 0516
Closed lunch
€

Osteria dell'Angelo
Via G. Bettolo 24
06 372 9470
Closed lunch (except Mon, Sat),
Sun
€

Pizzeria da Vittorio
Via S. Cosimato 14A
06 580 0353
Closed Sun
€

Bir & Fud
Via Benedetta 23
06 589 4016
€€

Meridionale
Via dei Fienaroli 30A
06 589 7196
Closed Mon
€€

Fine Dining

Sabatini
Vicolo di Santa Maria
in Trastevere 18
06 581 2026
€€€€€

Ferrara
Via del Moro 1A
06 580 3769
Closed lunch Mon-Sat
€€€€

Sora Lella
Via Ponte Quattro Capi 16
06 686 1601
€€€€€

Taverna dei Mercanti
Piazza de' Mercanti 3A
06 588 1693
€€

Antico Arco
Piazzale Aurelio 7
06 581 5274
€€€€

Il Ciak
Vicolo del Cinque 21
06 589 4774
Closed lunch Mon-Sat
€€

La Gensola
Piazza della Gensola 15
06 581 6312
Closed Sun in summer
€€€€

Il Matriciano
Via dei Gracchi 55
06 321 3040
Closed Wed (in winter),
Sat (in summer)
€€€

La Pergola
Rome Cavalieri Hilton Hotel,
Via Alberto Cadlolo 101
06 3509 2211
Open for dinner only, closed
Sun, Mon
€€€€€

Taberna de' Gracchi
Via dei Gracchi 266-268
06 321 3126
Closed Sun
€€€€€

Beyond the City Walls

Eataly
Piazzale XII Ottobre 1492
Metrò Piramide
06 9027 9201
Closed 15 Aug
€€€

Il Pulcino Ballerino
Via Degli Equi 66
06 494 1255
Disabled access
€€

Ristorante l'Archeologia, via Appia Antica
Via Appia Antica 139
Autobus 118
06 788 0494
Closed Tue
€€€€

La Villetta dal 1940, Piramide
Viale della Piramide Cestia 53
Bus 23, 30, 75, 95, 280, 716, 719
06 575 0597
€€

Primo al Pigneto
Via del Pigneto 46
06 701 3827
Closed Mon
€€€€

La Sibilla, Tivoli
Via della Sibilla 50
COTRAL bus from Ponte Mammolo
07 7433 5281
Closed Mon
€€

Ambaradam, Tarquinia
Piazza Matteotti 14
0766 857 073
Closed Wed
€€

Pinocchio, Frascati
Piazza del Mercato 21
Metrò Anagnina, then COTRAL bus
06 941 7883
Closed Mon-Fri lunch
€€

Scilla, Sperlonga
Via San Rocco 26
Train from Termini to Fondi, then bus
0771 549652
Closed Tue (in winter)
€€

Ristorante Enoteca La Torre, Viterbo
Via della Torre 5
COTRAL bus from Saxa Rubra or train from Roma Ostiense
0761 226467
Closed Sun dinner, Tue, Wed
€

WHERE TO STAY

Price range
For a standard, double room per night (with breakfast if included), taxes and extra charges.
– €   under 100 €
– €€   100 €-150 €
– €€€   150 €-250 €
– €€€€   250 €-350 €
– €€€€€   over 350 €
Unless otherwise stated, all hotels accept credit cards, have en-suite bathrooms and air conditioning.

Bastions of Luxury

Eden
Via Ludovisi 49
06 478 121
www.edenroma.com
Disabled access
€€€€€

Hassler
Piazza Trinità dei Monti 6
06 699 340
www.hotelhasslerroma.com
Disabled access
€€€€€

De Russie
Via del Babuino 9
06 328 881
www.roccofortecollection.it
Disabled access
€€€€€

St Regis Grand
Via V.E. Orlando 3
06 47091
www.thestregisgrandrome.com
Disabled access
€€€€€

Majestic
Via Veneto 50
06 421 441
www.rome-hotels-majestic.com
Disabled access
€€€€€

Regina Baglioni
Via Veneto 72
06 421 111
www.baglionihotels.com
Disabled access
€€€€€

De la Ville Intercontinental
Via Sistina 69
0800 1817341
www.ichotelsgroup.com
Disabled access
€€€€€

Gran Hotel Flora
Via Veneto 191
06 489 929
www.hotelfloraroma.com
Disabled access
€€€€€

Giulio Cesare
Via degli Scipioni 287
06 321 0751
www.hotelgiuliocesare.com
€€€€

Atlante Star
Via Vitelleschi 34
06 68638
www.atlantehotels.com
€€€€

Romantic Charmers

Westin Excelsior
Via Veneto 125
06 47081
www.starwoodhotels.com
Disabled access
€€€€€

Lord Byron
Via G. de Notaris 5
06 322 0404
www.lordbyronhotel.com
€€€€€

Raphael
Largo Febo 2
06 682 831
www.raphaelhotel.com
€€€€€

Caesar House Residenze Romane
Via Cavour 310
06 679 2674
www.caesarhouse.com
€€€

Farnese
Via Alessandro Farnese 30
06 321 2553
www.hotelfarnese.com
€€€€

Gran Hotel del Gianicolo
Viale delle Mura Gianicolensi 107
06 5833 5522
www.grandhotelgianicolo.it
Disabled access
€€€€

Hotel Piranesi
Via del Babuino 196
06 328041
www.hotelpiranesi.com
Disabled access
€€€€

Portrait Suites
Via Bocca di Leone 23
06 6938 0742
www.lungarnocollection.com
€€€€€

Crossing Condotti
Via Mario de' Fiori 28
06 699 20633
www.crossingcondotti.com
€€€

San Anselmo and Villa San Pio
Piazza S. Anselmo 2
and Via di Santa Melania
06 570 057
www.aventinohotels.com
€€€€

Comfort, Style and Value Hotels

Pantheon
Via dei Pastini 131
06 678 7746
www.hotelpantheon.com
Disabled access
€€€€

Dei Borgognoni
Via del Bufalo 126
06 6994 1505
www.hotelborgognoni.it
Disabled access
€€€€

Condotti
Via Mario de' Fiori 37
06 679 4661
www. hotelcondotti.com
€€€€

Cesàri
Via di Pietra 89A
06 674 9701
www.albergocesari.it
€€€

Fori Imperiali Cavalieri
Via Frangipane 34
06 679 6246
www.hotelforiimperiali.com
€€€

Tritone
Via del Tritone 210
06 699 22575
www.tritonehotel.com
€€€

Teatropace 33
Via del Teatro Pace 33
06 687 9075
www.hotelteatropace.com
€€€

Santa Chiara
Via Santa Chiara 21
06 687 2979
www.albergosantachiara.com
€€€€

Hotel Santa Maria
Vicolo del Piede 2
06 589 4626
www.htlsantamaria.com
Disabled access
€€€

Des Artistes
Via Villafranca 20
06 445 4365
www.hoteldesartistes.com
€€

Rooms with a View

Sole al Pantheon
Piazza della Rotonda 63
06 678 0441
www.hotelsolealpantheon.com
€€€€

Victoria
Via Campania 41
06 423 701
www.hotelvictoriaroma.com
Disabled access
€€€

Scalinata di Spagna
Piazza Trinità dei Monti 17
06 679 3006
www.hotelscalinata.com
Disabled access
€€€

Domus Aventina
Via di Santa Prisca 11B
06 574 6135
www.hoteldomusaventina.com
€€€

Teatro di Pompeo
Largo del Pallaro 8
06 683 00170
www.hotelteatrodipompeo.it
€€€

Sofitel Villa Borghese
Via Lombardia 47
06 478 021
www.sofitel.com
€€€€

Homs
Via della Vite 71-72
06 679 2976
www.hotelhoms.it
€€€€

Inn at the Spanish Steps
Via dei Condotti 85
06 699 25657
www.atspanishsteps.com
€€€€

Torre Colonna
Via delle Tre Cannelle 18
06 8360 0192
www.torrecolonna.it
€€€€

Abruzzi
Piazza della Rotonda 69
06 9784 1351
www.hotelabruzzi.it
€€€

Business Hotels

Boscolo Exedra
Piazza della Repubblica 47
06 4893 8012
www.exedra-roma.boscolohotel.it
€€€€€

Parco dei Principi
Via G. Frescobaldi 5
06 854 421
www.parcodeiprincipi.com
€€€€€

Grand Hotel Plaza
Via del Corso 126
06 6992 1111
www.grandhotelplaza.com
€€€€€

Cavalieri Hilton
Via Cadlolo 101
06 35091
www.romecavalieri.it
Disabled access
€€€€€

Mecenate Palace
Via Carlo Alberto 3
06 4470 2024
www.mecenatepalace.com
Disabled access
€€€€

Nazionale a Montecitorio
Piazza Montecitorio 131
06695001
www.hotelnazionale.it
Disabled access
€€€€€

Bernini Bristol
Piazza Barberini 23
06 488 931
www.berninibristol.com
Disabled access
€€€€€

Dei Consoli
Via Varrone 2
06 6889 2972
www.hoteldeiconsoli.com
Disabled access
€€€

Forum
Via Tor de' Conti 25-30
06 679 2446
www.hotelforumrome.com
€€€€

Radisson Blu es. Hotel
Via Turati 171
06 444 841
www.radissonblu.com/
eshotel-rome
Disabled access
€€€€€

Budget Gems

Sant'Anna
Borgo Pio 134
06 6880 1602
www.hotelsantanna.com
€€€

San Carlo
Via delle Carrozze 93
06 678 4548
www.hotelsancarloroma.com
€€€

Alimandi
Via Tunisi 1
06 3972 3941
www.alimandi.com
€€€

La Cisterna
Via della Cisterna 8
06 581 7212
www.cisternahotel.it
€€

Hotel Artorius
Via del Boschetto 13
06 482 1196
www.hotelartorius.com
Disabled access
€€

Al Centro di Roma B&B
Piazza Sant'Andrea della Valle 3
06 6813 5946
www.bbalcentrodiroma.com
€€

Campo de' Fiori
Via del Biscione 6
06 6880 6865
www.hotelcampodefiori.com
€€€

Carmel
Via Goffredo Mameli 11
06 580 9921
www.hotelcarmel.it
€€

Smeraldo
Vicolo dei Chiodaroli 9
06 687 5929
www.smeraldoroma.com
€€

Trastevere
Via L. Manara 24A-25
06 581 4713
www.hoteltrastevere.net
€€

Hostels and Religious Institutions

Colors
Via Boezio 31
06 687 4030
www.colorshotel.com
€

Blue Hostel
Via Carlo Alberto 13
340 925 8503
www.bluehostel.it
No credit cards
€

Orsa Maggiore for Women Only
Via San Francesco di Sales 1/A
06 689 3753
www.casainternazionaledella
donna.org
No air conditioning
€

Hostel Alessandro
and Alessandro Downtown
Via Vicenza 42 and Via Carlo
Cattaneo 23
06 446 1958/4434 0147
www.hostelsalessandro.com
Air conditioning
(Downtown only)
Disabled access
(Downtown only)
€

Pensione Ottaviano
Via Ottaviano 6
06 3973 8138
www.pensioneottaviano.com
No credit cards
No air conditioning
€

Hostel Sandy
Via Cavour 136
06 488 4585
www.sandyhostel.com
No credit cards
No air conditioning
€

Bed&Breakfast Cicerone 28
Via Cicerone 28
06 320 8195
www.romacicerone28.com
No credit cards
€

Agenzie di B&B
B&B Association of Rome
Via A. Pacinotti 73
06 5530 2248
www.b-b.rm.it
€

The Beehive
Via Marghera 8
06 4470 4553
www.the-beehive.com
€

Centro Diffusione Spiritualità
Via dei Riari 43-44
06 6880 6122
No credit cards
No air conditioning
€

Residences and Apartments

Santa Chiara
Via Santa Chiara 21
06 687 2979
www.albergosantachiara.com
€€€

Residence Palazzo al Velabro
Via del Velabro 16
06 679 2758
www.velabro.it
Disabled access
€€€

Aldrovandi Residence
Via Aldrovandi 11
Tram 19
06 322 1430
www.aldrovandiresidence.it
Disabled access
€€

Residenza Farnese
Via del Mascherone 59
06 6821 0980
www.residenzafarneseroma.it
€€€

Residenza di Ripetta
Via di Ripetta 231
06 323 1144
www.ripetta.it
Disabled access
€€€€

Trastevere
Via L. Manara 24A-25
06 581 4713
www.hoteltrastevere.net
€

Retrome
Via Marco Aurelio 47
06 9555 7334
www.retrome.net
€€

Vatican Suites
Villa Tassoni
Viale Medaglie d'Oro 138
06 355 899
www.tassoni.it
Vatican Suites
Via Nicolò V 5
06 633 306
www.vatican-suites.com
€€

Aurelia Residence San Pietro
Via Vittoria 60-64
06 6992 5834
www.residencevittoria.com
No credit cards
€€€€

Apartment Rentals
At@Home
Via del Corso 300
06 3212 0102
www.at-home-italy.com
Rome Sweet Home
06 6992 4091
www.romesweethome.it
€

Cross-Pollinate
06 9028 8130
www.crosspollinate.com
€

Photograph Credits
All the images are
by Giovanni Rinaldi
except:

© Shutterstock:
alessandro0770 p. 53
Annto pp. 94, 118
Anshar pp. 38–39
Bepsy pp. 82–83
Cora Mueller pp. 104–105
Cortyn pp. 2, 76–77
Giuseppe Lancia pp. 120–121
Maurizio Biso p. 109
Mlkhailo p. 99
Muzhik p. 112
Pablo Debat p. 33
Pisaphotography pp. 60–61
S. Borisov pp. 6–7
Styve Reineck pp. 20–21
Tramont_ana pp. 126–127

By kind permission of the
Ministero dei beni e delle attività
culturali e del turismo /
Soprintendenza speciale per
il Colosseo, il Museo Nazionale
Romano e l'area archeologica
di Roma

By kind permission of the
Sovrintendenza Capitolina ai Beni
Culturali

The publisher can be contacted
by entitled parties for any
iconographic sources that have
not been identified.

ISO 9001
Mondadori Electa S.p.A. is certified for the
Quality Management System by Bureau Veritas Italia S.p.A.,
in compliance with UNI EN ASO 9001: 2008.

This book respects the environment
The paper used was produced using wood from forests managed to strict
environmental standards; the companies involved guarantee sustainable
production certified environmentally.

Design
Cdm associati Udine

Translation
Richard Sadleir

The hotel and restaurant addresses featured in this book were taken from
the *Top 10 Roma* guide, with the kind permission of Dorling Kinderlsey Ltd
www.dk.com

This volume was printed at Elcograf S.p.A.,
via Mondadori 15, Verona in 2016

Printed in Italy